CONTENTS

JEAN DESRAVINES | BENJAMIN FENTON

with Lori Taliaferro Riddick

THE SCHOOL LEADERSHIP PLAYBOOK

A FIELD GUIDE FOR DRAMATIC IMPROVEMENT

New Leaders

JOSSEY-BASS™

A Wiley Brand

Published by Jossey-Bass
A Wiley Brand
One Montgomery Street, Suite 1000, San Francisco, CA 94104-4594—www.josseybass.com

Jossey-Bass books and products are available through most bookstores. To contact Jossey-Bass directly call our Customer Care Department within the U.S. at 800-956-7739, outside the U.S. at 317-572-3986, or fax 317-572-4002.

Wiley publishes in a variety of print and electronic formats and by print-on-demand. Some material included with standard print versions of this book may not be included in e-books or in print-on-demand. If this book refers to media such as a CD or DVD that is not included in the version you purchased, you may download this material at http://booksupport.wiley.com. For more information about Wiley products, visit www.wiley.com.

Library of Congress Cataloging-in-Publication Data is on file.

ISBN 978-1-119-04421-5 (paper)
ISBN 978-1-119-04405-5 (ebk.)
ISBN 978-1-119-04425-3 (ebk.)
Printed in the United States of America

FIRST EDITION

PB Printing   10 9 8 7 6 5 4 3 2 1

ABOUT THE AUTHORS

Jean Desravines serves as chief executive officer of New Leaders, an innovative school reform organization that develops and supports highly effective leaders to turn around the nation's high-need public schools. Jean has more than fifteen years of leadership experience in education and community development, with a primary focus on improving outcomes for kids in underserved communities. Before joining New Leaders, Jean served as senior counselor to the chancellor of New York City's public school system, the executive director for the Office of Parent and Community Engagement, chief of staff to the senior counselor for Education Policy, and director for Community Relations at the New York City Department of Education.

Jean serves as a board member for 100Kin10, his alma mater St. Francis College, and St. Benedict's College Prep in Newark, New Jersey. He served on Governor Andrew M. Cuomo's Education Reform Commission and was named to *Forbes*'s "Impact 30," recognizing the world's leading social entrepreneurs. Jean is a graduate of St. Francis College and New York University, where he was the recipient of the Dean's Scholarship.

Benjamin Fenton is cofounder and chief strategy officer at New Leaders. A recognized expert on principal quality, Ben leads New Leaders' human capital consulting initiatives, helping states and districts develop new policies and practices for principal evaluation and principal effectiveness. He is also responsible for the ongoing implementation of the New Leaders research agenda and programmatic evaluation. He co-led the development of New Leaders' Transformational Leadership Framework, identifying the school practices and principal actions found in high-gaining, high-poverty public schools.

Ben is also a founding board member of Teach Plus, a nonprofit dedicated to retaining and developing great teachers who improve student achievement. He formerly worked as a consultant at McKinsey & Company, focusing on marketing and operational efficiency. Ben is a graduate of Harvard College and the Harvard Business School, where he received the Fiske award for excellence in teaching in the Economics Department.

Lori Taliaferro Riddick is executive director of policy and practice services at New Leaders. Lori leads New Leaders' district-level human capital consulting initiatives, helping districts develop and implement new approaches to principal evaluation and principal effectiveness. In addition to developing principal evaluation models, Lori facilitates professional learning experiences, leads communities of practice, and provides coaching for assistant superintendents to improve the quality of principal support to all schools in the district. Lori also supports turnaround principals who are tasked with improving student outcomes.

Lori led New Leaders' Transformational Leadership Framework qualitative research project and co-led the development of the subsequent framework, identifying the school practices and principal actions found in high-gaining, high-poverty public schools. Lori is a graduate of the University of Pennsylvania, where she received a BA in urban studies and an MS in education.

ABOUT NEW LEADERS

New Leaders ↗ FOUNDED IN 2000 BY A TEAM OF SOCIAL entrepreneurs, New Leaders is a national nonprofit that develops transformational school leaders and designs effective leadership policies and practices for school systems across the country.

Research shows—and our experience confirms—that strong school leaders have a powerful multiplier effect, dramatically improving the quality of teaching and raising student achievement in a school.

We have trained more than sixteen hundred leaders nationwide and have impacted over 350,000 students. Students in New Leaders schools consistently achieve at higher levels than their peers, have higher high school graduation rates, and are making progress in closing the achievement gap.

As New Leaders enters its second decade, we are broadening our work in order to reach more students with greater impact. Beyond training new principals, we are now developing transformative leaders throughout schools and school systems—from teacher leaders and assistant principals to veteran principals and district supervisors. We are also working with school systems to build the kinds of policies and practices that allow strong leaders to succeed in driving academic excellence for students.

Access the Bonus Web Videos

The companion web page for this book includes a number of videos showing effective school leaders demonstrating some of the principal actions from the Playbook. To access these videos, go to the publisher's website at www.wiley.com/go/slplaybook and use the password **44215**.

LEADERSHIP FOR SCHOOL IMPROVEMENT

NEW LEADERS' MISSION IS TO ENSURE THAT all students in our country's public schools receive an excellent education that puts them on the path to success in college and life.

We know that effective teachers improve student learning; thus it is critical that we both identify and retain top teachers in our schools. Yet the only way to ensure that children have great teachers every day, in every classroom, every year is by making sure that at the helm of every school is a great leader who attracts, supports, motivates, and retains high-quality teachers.

Research shows that principals are a high-impact lever in transforming schools. More than a decade of research supports principals' critical role in shaping the quality of teaching and learning at the school level.[1] Some 97 percent of teachers say that great leadership is very important for keeping good teachers in their school. On average, a principal accounts for 25 percent of a school's total impact on student achievement—significant for a single individual. Indeed, the difference between an average and an above-average principal can impact student achievement by as much as 20 percentage points.[2] The influence of

....
1 See, for example, Leithwood, Louis, Anderson, and Wahlstrom, 2004; Marzano, Waters, and McNulty, 2005.

an individual principal can be quite substantial,[3] especially in low-performing schools, where improvement does not occur without strong leadership.[4]

Although principals can impact student achievement directly, they typically have a more indirect impact by influencing school practices and culture. Recently, research has suggested that the primary way principals impact student achievement is by improving teacher effectiveness.[5] There has been much debate in the research over whether principals improve teacher effectiveness through management decisions, workplace satisfaction, or direct efforts to improve instruction. A long tradition of research on instructional leadership argues that schools effective in improving student achievement have principals who focus on curriculum and instruction.[6] More recent research has found that principals have a substantial effect on student achievement by structuring how teachers work together to promote each other's learning.[7] Another line of research suggests that the primary means through which principals improve student achievement is through hiring, evaluating, and removing teachers.[8] Yet another argues that principals have the most impact when they create a climate that improves retention of effective teachers.[9] We believe that bringing together these many pieces is the work of successful school leaders.

. . . .

2 Marzano et al., 2005.
3 Branch, Hanushek, and Rivkin, 2012.
4 Aladjem et al., 2010; Bryk, Sebring, Allensworth, Luppescu, and Easton, 2010; Louis, Leithwood, Wahlstrom, and Anderson, 2010.
5 Branch et al., 2012; Louis et al., 2010; Supovitz, Sirinides, and May, 2010.
6 Fink and Resnick, 2001.
7 Louis et al., 2010; Supovitz et al., 2010.
8 Rice, 2010.
9 Chenoweth and Theokas, 2011; Ladd, 2009; Louis et al., 2010.

OUR EXPERIENCE: DEVELOPING TRANSFORMATIONAL LEADERS FOR HIGH-POVERTY SCHOOLS

New Leaders was founded in 2000 to confront the changing demands and requirements of the principalship, as well as the growing recognition that schools need to adapt their practices to effectively prepare students for successful entry to college and careers. In the past fifteen years, we have trained more than sixteen hundred leaders in urban systems. This year, our leaders are working with more than 350,000 students across fifteen districts and in more than one hundred charter schools. We base our work on the belief that all children can achieve academic success and on clear evidence that effective school leaders are the key to dramatic school improvement. In service to our mission, we partner with low-performing, high-need urban school districts struggling to meet the needs of all their children.

Principals trained by New Leaders have driven remarkable student achievement gains in district and charter settings, shedding light on the critical need for a larger pipeline of school leadership talent and a more equitable distribution of effective principals.

The RAND Corporation recently released the results of a seven-year independent, external evaluation that, by controlling for other factors, determined the impact a New Leaders principal has on student achievement. RAND found that students attending New Leaders schools outperform their peers specifically because they have a New Leaders principal.

Our work with leaders across contexts uniquely positions us to share our research, learning, and insights about how to successfully transform and sustain urban schools.

⏣ THE TRANSFORMATIONAL LEADERSHIP FRAMEWORK

New Leaders developed the Transformational Leadership Framework (TLF) to pinpoint *what* schools achieving significant student academic gains were doing and *how* they were doing it. Looking at school systems across the country, we noticed a puzzling pattern: leaders with similar values, similar training, and similar approaches to leadership were having noticeably different results. Some were successful in transforming school performance, whereas others led schools that demonstrated only moderate increases in student achievement. We wanted to understand what distinguished these principals who had been equipped with similar tool kits: What actions were the leaders taking in schools making significant improvements? How were schoolwide practices being implemented?

Through extensive research over the past six years, we have identified a set of common actions and practices that cross grade levels, school size, and geographies, and captured those actions within the TLF. As a result of this work, we have adjusted our approach to leadership development and are eager to share our learning with other like-minded educators working to improve the opportunities available to all children. We believe that schools implementing these actions will see the transformative success necessary to drive significant gains in student achievement and will be able to close the achievement gap.

> **New Leaders developed the TLF to pinpoint *what* schools achieving significant student academic gains were doing and *how* they were doing it.**

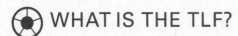 WHAT IS THE TLF?

The TLF is an easy-to-use "field guide" for all educators to assess current practices and support school transformation. The framework centers around five categories that effective schools focus on to improve and maintain school performance:

- Learning and Teaching

- School Culture

- Talent Management

- Operations and Planning

- Personal Leadership

The first two categories define the two primary drivers of student achievement: rigorous, data-driven learning and teaching, and a belief-based school culture. The **Learning and Teaching** category outlines actions required to develop and implement the content and instructional strategies needed to improve academic offerings and student performance. The **School Culture** category describes the values, expectations, and supports that inspire and guide staff and students toward increased success.

Two additional categories of a principal's work are essential to supporting these drivers: **Talent Management** describes the essential role other members of the team play in creating and sustaining schoolwide change, and **Operations and Planning** outlines the seamless structures that support the team's work to put the vision in place.

Undergirding all of these categories is that of **Personal Leadership**. This category comprises the types of leadership modeled by a principal who sets the tone for all student and adult relationships and practices in the school.

Note that in effective schools—those whose students achieve consistent academic growth—each of the categories function interdependently and cannot stand alone. For the purposes of this book, however, we explain each separately.

Structure of the TLF

Each of the five categories is described from the broadest view of a leader's efforts, which we call **levers**—down to the specific **actions** that principals and school teams implement to improve student performance. Each action is divided into specific **principal actions** that principals and **leadership team** members must take and **school actions** that result from these principal actions. School actions are the consistent and observable actions of staff, students, and families within the school community that lead to improvements in student outcomes. Together these pieces describe the effect that well-applied leadership actions can bring about.

Here is one example of how the framework flows, taken from an actual sequence within the TLF.

CATEGORY: Operations and Systems
Lever 3: Budget

ACTION 2: External Partnerships

PRINCIPAL ACTIONS	SCHOOL ACTION
Review existing community partnerships to assess their current impact on the school Introduce partners to the school's priority areas and to ensure alignment between partner and school	Criteria are established to review and identify partnerships, including alignment to the strategic priorities and identified student support needs of the school

PRINCIPAL ACTIONS	SCHOOL ACTION
If partners are unable to adapt to focus on high priority areas reframe, eliminate, or replace the partnership	

Stages of Development

In our study of high-poverty schools that were able to make and sustain student outcome gains, we found that schools implemented a similar set of actions over time and in sequence. They did not immediately become highly effective in all areas. Instead, the schools we studied demonstrated a similar pattern of new actions implemented over time. We have described these patterns and sequences of school actions as stages of school development—or "stages"—in our Transformational Leadership Framework.

The TLF is therefore broken into stages, to help guide principals on where their schools are in their work in different areas, from instruction to school culture to talent management. For schools in need of major changes in several key areas, the framework offers help in determining where and, more important, how to begin. By examining the actions they and their school staff and community are—or are not—implementing around instruction, culture, and so on, principals can pinpoint the highest-leverage actions they and their school community can take to better position their school for making sustained improvement in student achievement.

As leaders assess the current state of their schools, there are some common characteristics that are observable in specific stages.

In Stage 1, schools develop consistent systems and basic structures in such areas as classroom routines, student behavioral expectations, and teacher observation. These systems and structures move the school from being unfocused and even chaotic to having clear expectations and staff practices across the school. This transition to Stage 1 is particularly important for turnaround schools or schools in significant need of improvement, where these systems and structures are rarely in place. In terms of leadership approach, principals in schools developing Stage 1 practices have to establish and monitor clear expectations and nonnegotiable outcomes for staff and students. As an example, the leader may work collaboratively with the staff to develop a short list of consistent student behavioral expectations and staff responses, but the principal would set the expectation that once established, these expectations and responses must be implemented consistently by every staff member. The principal would spend significant time in Stage 1 monitoring consistency of implementation and reinforcing this transition to consistent systems.

In Stage 2, schools develop greater rigor and differentiation to meet student needs, not only in instructional content and strategies but also in the use of data, in supports and structures for building school culture, and in staff development and professional learning. In Stage 2, a school leadership team of other administrators and teacher leaders with a strong shared vision provides for expanded leadership capacity across the TLF categories.

In Stage 3, schools develop a deep sense of ownership, across staff, students, and families, of the key practices of the school. Because nearly every member of the school community is invested in these practices and has the capacity to implement them at a consistently high level, the school is able to sustain high levels of student outcomes, even through staff and leadership transitions.

It is important to note that the stages are not necessarily permanent—it is possible for a school to regress to an earlier stage in an action or category in the face of ineffective leadership, changes to leadership, staff turnover, or decisions that dismantle systems or structures.

Our studies showed that as the schools successfully implemented most of the school actions in a particular stage, they demonstrated significant improvements in student outcomes. For example, when schools moved from being places lacking in basic systems and expectations to become communities that exhibited the school actions identified in Stage 1, they often saw initial improvements in student achievement. However, when schools maintained Stage 1 practices but did not adapt their actions to develop Stage 2 practices, we found that their student outcomes often reached a plateau. This helped explain a consistent finding of other research on high-poverty schools—namely, that schools can make rapid initial improvements in student outcomes, but

> Note that the stages are not necessarily permanent—it is possible for a school to regress to an earlier stage in an action or category in the face of ineffective leadership, changes to leadership, staff turnover, or decisions that dismantle systems or structures.

then struggle to sustain these outcomes or to continue this pace of improvement.

More important, this concept of stages of development has provided stronger guidance for leaders entering schools in significant need of improvement. Although these leaders are often familiar with the research around high-performing schools, including high-performing high-poverty schools, the gap that they see upon entry between those research-based practices and the current state of the school can seem nearly impossible to overcome. The TLF provides a clearer trajectory indicating where to start the improvement process in such schools, and serves as an ongoing guide to leaders who want to diagnose the current state of their schools and continue making improvements toward high and sustained levels of student outcomes.

Putting the Framework to Use

This framework is not an exhaustive list of all the things a principal must do, nor should it serve as a rubric or checklist for principal evaluations. Instead, the TLF functions best as a tool to help leaders diagnose the current state of their school practices and then identify the highest-leverage principal actions to take given that diagnosis. As part of the diagnostic process, school leaders can not only review the trajectory and details around student outcomes data but also use the framework to identify what stage of school practices is evident in the school within each key lever of the TLF. For example, the principal might find that most of her school's practices fall into Stage 1, but that there are a few key levers where the school has still not succeeded in implementing the basic Stage 1 practices consistently. She would then choose to focus heavily on those lagging practices before initiating a general push to move all key levers to Stage 2 practices.

We have found that in conducting such a diagnosis, school leaders sometimes jump to judgments in two ways that can distract them from a deeper review of school practices. First, leaders may make judgments about the current stage of school practices based solely on student outcomes data. However, in order to make substantial and sustained improvements in outcomes, leaders must look further to the details of school practices that underlie these outcomes. Second, school leaders sometimes assume that all school practices fall into a single stage across all key levers, and may refer informally to their school as a "Stage 2 school." Although these practices often do flow together and are at similar stages, the best diagnoses of school practices identify the few key levers where practices are at a different stage, allowing for effective plans to improve in those targeted areas.

As we mentioned earlier, although the TLF may resemble principal evaluation tools used by some school systems, we do not recommend using the TLF for that purpose. Whatever the outcomes of a school diagnosis, evaluating a school's practices within each key lever as a Stage 1, 2, or 3 practice should not be understood as an evaluation of the school leader. Many principals enter challenging turnaround school environments where every lever is in Stage 1, or not yet even at Stage 1. In these situations, it takes a skilled leader to diagnose and lead improvements in school practices from chaos to Stage 1, and then forward over

> **This framework is not an exhaustive list of all the things a principal must do, nor should it serve as a rubric or checklist for principal evaluations.**

time to Stage 2 and Stage 3. New Leaders thinks of great principals as not only those who lead Stage 3 schools but also those who, from any starting point, can identify the highest-impact areas for change and make dramatic improvements in student outcomes as they lead improvements to the next stage.

The TLF has allowed principals in the New Leaders community to propel their schools to greater gains in student achievement. We are excited to be able to share this field guide broadly so that other educators can benefit from using this tool to assess current practices, identify strategies, and improve student performance.

NOTE

All bolded words in the framework are defined in the Glossary.

Learning and Teaching

THE LEARNING AND TEACHING CATEGORY DESCRIBES STRATEGIES and practices adults can use to plan for and provide the content necessary to prepare students for college.

As we have learned from our experience in selecting, training, and supporting leaders, highly effective principals work with their teachers to improve the quality of instruction through four levers:

- Aligning curriculum to both state and college-readiness standards

- Ensuring consistent and high-quality classroom practices, routines, and instructional strategies

- Utilizing diverse student-level data to drive instructional improvement

- Focusing on student-centered instruction

In schools that are improving student achievement rates, leaders and their teams work to ensure that research-based curriculum and instruction align to the specific learning goals of their students, while working to help students meet and exceed expectations. Using either district-level or school-created curriculum, these schools work to develop common definitions of rigor that are well understood throughout the building and are translated into rigorous units of study that guide the day-to-day planning of teachers.

Over time, *how* students are taught is increasingly consistent across classrooms, teachers improve their planning to maximize instructional time, and instruction is designed to meet the needs of individual students while not compromising expectations.

In schools that are improving student achievement rates, leaders and their teams work to ensure that research-based curriculum and instruction align to the specific learning goals of their students, while working to help students meet and exceed expectations.

TRANSFORMATIONAL PRINCIPALS IN ACTION

Claudette Yarbrough

To align instruction across classrooms, all new and returning teachers at Higgs, Carter, King Gifted & Talented Charter Academy in San Antonio, Texas, participated in a learning session focused on schoolwide routines for organizing and planning lessons and on classroom management of students. Principal Claudette Yarbrough set the agenda and led much of the training herself. Yarbrough said that because she was personally involved, she could "make sure that the teachers know what I expect them to know. I know what gets said in the training and what we train on, so I can hold people accountable." Throughout the training, Yarbrough employed techniques and activities that she expected teachers to employ in the classroom with their students. She said, "In the school's first several years, I didn't lead the summer training. I just planned it. But I saw that many teachers still didn't know what was expected of them after the training. There had been too much telling and explaining during the training sessions and not enough good teaching. Teachers had been told what to do, but not shown how to do it. My goal now is to model the kind of teaching we expect to see in our classrooms."

Teachers also modify instruction based on ongoing review of data generated by student work, checks for understanding, assessments, and projects.

TRANSFORMATIONAL PRINCIPALS IN ACTION

Tatiana Epanchin-Troyan

New Leader Principal Tatiana Epanchin-Troyan of Monarch Academy in Oakland, California, realized that having teacher teams analyze data together set a collegial and supportive environment where teachers could look to their peers for ideas on how to teach content, so she established a system of convening grade-level team meetings that facilitate meaningful collaboration within her teacher teams. Their grade-level meetings, called Data Talks, are structured conversations during which teachers work together to analyze students' formative and interim assessment data to track mastery of content and skills. To support high-quality conversations that are driven by data, Epanchin-Troyan developed and shared a common set of protocols for analyzing student data and targeting instruction based on the findings. During the Data Talks, teachers are expected to offer each other support in analyzing the data to determine where the weaknesses are and to give advice on developing strategies to address those needs.

Students who have not yet mastered content are given extra support in small groups during class time and are referred to additional tiers of intervention as needed. These interventions buoy students who are performing below grade level, so as to facilitate their ability to make more than one year of progress.

Throughout the Learning and Teaching category, we describe how these four levers support instruction that prepares students for success in the twenty-first century.

Learning and Teaching Category Map

| **Lever 1:**
 Aligned Curriculum | **Lever 2: Classroom**
 Practices and Instruction |

Curriculum is aligned to both state and college-readiness standards

Consistently high-quality classroom practices, routines, and instructional strategies are in place

| **Actions** | **Actions** |

- **Scope and Sequence:** Articulate clear sequence of key learning outcomes across grade levels aligned to standards
- **Units of Study:** Plan effectively to translate curriculum into lessons and units with clear objectives, activities, strategies, and assessments aligned to the standards

- **Classroom Practices:** Implement effective procedures, routines, and practices that support and facilitate student learning
- **Instructional Strategies:** Match instructional methods to student need and use them consistently to improve student engagement, student performance, and development of critical thinking skills

Lever 3: Data

Schools utilize diverse student-level data to drive instructional improvement

Actions

- **Data Collection and Analysis:** Collect and analyze multiple sources of data to track and assess student progress
- **Continuum of Assessments:** Develop learning targets using multiple assessments aligned to standards, to inform student grouping and adjust curriculum pacing
- **Feedback on Progress:** Provide multiple opportunities to discuss progress toward goals with students

Lever 4: Student-Centered Interventions

Schools develop student-centered instruction that meets all students' learning needs

Actions

- **Interventions, Preventions, and Accelerations:** Put in place a pyramid of support for students below grade level, and preventions for students at risk; create expanded learning opportunities for those who have attained proficiency

LEVER 1: Aligned curriculum

Note: Some of these actions may be addressed at the district level rather than at the school level. In cases where parts of this work are completed at the central office level, it is important for the school leader and team to review and ensure that school staff have a shared understanding of the standards, the curriculum framework, and expectations of rigor.

PRINCIPAL ACTIONS	
STAGE 1	Articulate a common definition of rigor in order to develop a shared understanding of what rigorous student work looks like in every course and grade
	Ensure that **curriculum maps** clearly recommend pacing and address standards for each grade level and content area
	Identify and address gaps between written, taught, and tested curriculum
	Lead an analysis of the standards with the **instructional leadership team** to identify learning targets, curricular activities, and performance tasks that will inform units of study
STAGE 2	Analyze the curriculum and standards to ensure vertical alignment of content across all grades and subject areas
	Build capacity of teacher teams to analyze and align standards, curricula, instructional strategies, and assessment tools
	Ensure that curriculum teaches students how to use the process of inquiry to solve complex problems
	Ensure that interim and formative assessments are aligned to the standards
	(High school) Intentionally increase the number of opportunities for students to participate in Advanced Placement and honors-level courses
STAGE 3	Lead annual review process in which staff collaborate to assess alignment to college readiness standards across grades
	Ensure that curriculum requires students to routinely address and engage with complex integrated problems

ACTION 1: Scope and Sequence

SCHOOL ACTIONS
Teachers, staff, and students work toward a common definition of rigor aligned to the vision **Scope and sequence** is broken into units, and assessments are aligned to grade-level standards as defined by the state assessment or state standards A curriculum map delineates key ideas, essential questions, and several recommended texts for each unit
Vertical alignment allows users to see how skills connect and **scaffold** across grade levels Grade-level and content teams review the standards together to analyze what students would need to *know* to demonstrate mastery of each standard and what students would need to *be able to do* to demonstrate mastery of a standard Teams analyze similarities and differences between these expectations and what is currently taught in the curriculum (High school) Admittance policies and entrance criteria for AP and honors classes are reviewed to ensure that all students have access to rigorous content
Staff demonstrate a shared understanding of how standards translate to rigorous expectations of student work, and ensure that they are defining mastery consistently Teachers find opportunities to surpass the state standards to require higher levels of learning that will lead to college and career success

LEVER 1: Aligned curriculum

PRINCIPAL ACTIONS
STAGE 1 Articulate clear expectations for common planning time and create standard unit planning and lesson planning templates
Model effective approaches to unit planning and regularly review unit plans to provide teacher teams with feedback on their plans
Review the curriculum materials to ensure that they are aligned to the curriculum and lesson plans
Create and institute criteria for making judgments about the instructional design of curriculum materials
(High school) Offer courses that support development of **twenty-first-century skills** and dismantle tracking practices that prevent some groups of students from participating in college preparatory classes
STAGE 2 Lead staff in creating high-quality lesson plans that consistently include **differentiation, reteaching**, and formative assessment
Develop capacity of the instructional leadership team to review unit and lesson plans for alignment and rigor
Lead teachers in planning for curriculum units that align to the state and college-readiness standards and build their capacity to review and assess lesson quality
Implement common expectations of rigor and ensure that all staff understand how it applies to specific subject areas
Make certain the curriculum materials match to all areas of the curriculum and ensure access to materials that are culturally relevant for all students
STAGE 3 Ensure that all curriculum materials include rigorous content and require students to apply knowledge
Ensure that staff are actively looking for connections between content areas

ACTION 2: Units of Study

SCHOOL ACTIONS
Unit and lesson plans are developed by teacher teams and reviewed on a regular basis
All lesson plans include clear objectives, opening activities, multiple paths of instruction to a clearly defined curricular goal, and formative assessments
All materials are examined for clarity of purpose and relevance to students
Systems are in place to ensure that lesson and unit plans are written and reviewed on a set schedule All unit plans include regular formative assessments of student learning Teacher teams have deep and frequent conversations about formative student data and strategies to adjust instruction for every student Students develop the skills to engage in complex problems through a process of inquiry, discovery, and self-questioning to solve complex problems Grade-level and content-area teams review curriculum materials to ensure that they align to the standards and support the development of critical thinking skills Unit and lesson plans consistently include cognitively challenging tasks, and classroom instruction demonstrates connection to students' lives Systems are in place to ensure that lesson and unit plans are aligned to the scope and sequence
Staff work to ensure that students know the necessary content to successfully transition from elementary school to middle school and from middle school to high school Curriculum materials and maps are revised quarterly based on student achievement results

LEVER 2: Classroom practices and instruction

	PRINCIPAL ACTIONS
STAGE 1	Identify, teach, and consistently monitor three to five consistent classroom procedures, routines, and practices that support student learning
	Ensure that every staff member has the skills to implement the identified procedures, routines, and practices
	Monitor the implementation of the three to five nonnegotiable routines and practices
STAGE 2	Review and revise procedures, routines, and practices based on student learning data
STAGE 3	Monitor and reinforce the routines and practices regularly

ACTION 1: Classroom Practices

SCHOOL ACTIONS
Classrooms share some common procedures, routines, and practices
Staff maximize learning by using transition time effectively
Instructional time is maximized through consistent and efficient structures for: class opening, homework collection, within-class transitions, and formative assessments
New staff and students are introduced to shared practices and routines
Students lead and facilitate schoolwide practices
All teachers and students implement the schoolwide classroom practices and routines consistently and with quality

LEVER 2: Classroom practices and instruction

	PRINCIPAL ACTIONS
STAGE 1	Assess instructional strategies currently being implemented across grades and classrooms for alignment to student needs and standards
	Identify three to five instructional focus areas and instructional strategies that focus on intentional and explicit teaching of critical thinking skills
	Lead schoolwide professional development that focuses on creating meaningful learning experiences that lead to mastery
	Observe staff regularly to provide implementation support as needed
	Periodically monitor alignment between plans and classroom practices
STAGE 2	Ensure that staff are differentiating instruction to meet all students' needs and to ensure that all students master content
	Monitor and make adjustments to the instructional strategies on the basis of student progress
STAGE 3	Systematically and regularly review the effectiveness of instructional strategies
	Model effective instructional strategies and provide feedback to teachers about the implementation of instructional strategies

ACTION 2: Instructional Strategies

SCHOOL ACTIONS
All staff participate in schoolwide professional development to learn and practice high-leverage instructional strategies
Classroom instruction builds conceptual understanding, procedural skills, and fluency, and gives time for practice and application
Students are aware of the learning outcomes for most lessons
Students are regularly asked to defend their positions and to debate with others
Teachers consistently use a variety of instructional strategies to differentiate content based on student learning needs
Students have frequent opportunities to lead through peer teaching
Students understand the ideas specified in the standards and draw on them in a variety of contexts
Classroom instruction incorporates high-quality experiences of rigorous dialogue and critical thinking skills
Students recognize and understand the importance of content that is taught
Students use problem-solving strategies in a variety of settings

LEVER 3: Data

		PRINCIPAL ACTIONS
STAGE 1		Determine the most important student learning data points, including attendance and discipline, that will drive decisions, and use that data to make decisions
		Hold regular meetings with teacher teams to review student work and other forms of student-level data
		Explicitly link conversations about assessment to conversations about how to change instructional practice
		(High school) Build initial systems to track attendance, grades, and credit earning for secondary students to identify early **"off track"** warning signs
STAGE 2		Develop and support staff ability to analyze data and to use that data to identify and prioritize student needs, guide student grouping, and design **reteaching** strategies
		Provide evidence of progress and student work toward an established goal when giving feedback to staff
		Create **action plans** for whole-school professional development with and for teachers in order to address any learning gaps that exist across classrooms
STAGE 3		Make every instructional and student support decision using evidence of student progress
		Hold teachers accountable for knowing how their students are progressing
		Hold teachers accountable for using multiple sources of student learning data during common planning, classroom observations, and observation debriefs

ACTION 1: Data Collection and Analysis

SCHOOL ACTIONS
Student data is shared with all relevant staff
Staff have data on the achievement gap in their school and utilize that data to intentionally prioritize closing it
(High school) Performance of secondary students is tracked closely throughout the school year to ensure that they remain "**on track**" to graduate in four years
Every teacher differentiates instruction and/or reteaches key concepts on the basis of formative student achievement data
A continuous data review process is in place (including aligning assessments, analyzing interim and formative assessments, and taking action based on results through corrective instruction and other strategies) to ensure that student misconceptions are addressed through instruction and students learn taught material
The instructional leadership team reviews disaggregated data to track and monitor the progress of all students and provide evidence-based feedback to teachers
Teacher teams frequently analyze data for root causes; on the basis of this analysis, students are regrouped and targeted, and the curricular scope and sequence is revisited throughout the school year
Teachers track the learning of every student using multiple measures to determine individualized student goals and plans

LEVER 3: Data

	PRINCIPAL ACTIONS
STAGE 1	Ensure that staff are looking at multiple measures to assess student progress, including informal checks for understanding and performance tasks
	Implement an ongoing common interim assessment cycle and ensure a quick (forty-eight-hour) turnaround of data so that leading data trends and gaps in learning are used to guide decisions
	Analyze interim assessments for alignment to state standards and written curriculum; if interim assessments are not available, select or develop an assessment that is aligned with state standards and written curriculum
STAGE 2	Train staff in the effective development of rigorous performance tasks that truly assess mastery, particularly against the state and college-readiness standards
	Set the expectation and provide time for teachers to develop larger projects and rubrics for assessing mastery
	Observe and provide feedback on corrective instruction to support effective use of data
STAGE 3	Implement a comprehensive student assessment process that creates common expectations for corrective instruction action planning
	Carefully select assessment items to align to the level of cognitive rigor associated with a given learning target or standard

ACTION 2: Continuum of Assessments

Interim assessments are given three to four times per year to determine if students learned what was taught, and time for corrective instruction is built into the scope and sequence

Teachers review assessments at the beginning of each interim assessment cycle and use evidence to predict student performance

Interim assessments are aligned to college-readiness standards

Instructional decisions throughout the year, including student grouping/differentiation and interventions, are based on interim, daily, and weekly formative assessments

In addition to regular interim assessments, teachers use multiple assessments to inform instruction and guide corrective instruction

Students track their own goals and progress data, know their current level of proficiency, and receive frequent feedback on their performance and on areas of improvement

Teachers use a corrective instruction action planning process to identify trends in student misconceptions, identify why students may not have learned the concept, and create a revised approach to instruction and assessment using the data

Teacher teams have deep and frequent conversations about formative student data and about strategies to adjust instruction for every student

(High school) School staff review college acceptance, matriculation, persistence, and graduation data to improve schoolwide learning and teaching, culture, and college supports

LEVER 3: Data

		PRINCIPAL ACTIONS
STAGE 1		Create expectations for assessing progress toward proficiency and specified actions
		Build a practice whereby students are given frequent feedback on their work, including clearly outlined areas for improvement
		Establish grading practices and summative judgments that align to learning targets
STAGE 2		Define and implement a feedback policy that focuses on specific criteria for success
		Require teachers to separate the consequences for missing time or work from the assessment of mastery or progress toward goals
		Implement a standards-based grading policy characterized by the attainment of learning targets
STAGE 3		Build inter-rater reliability so that assessment of student work and student progress is consistent across classrooms
		Create systems to make daily or weekly grades visible to families

ACTION 3: Feedback on Progress

SCHOOL ACTIONS
Staff understand criteria for mastery of specific tasks
Summative assessments and grades are given after multiple rounds of feedback
Expectations and criteria for grade-level proficiency and mastery are consistent and known by all
Feedback is specific and helps students understand and correct their mistakes and misconceptions
Summative assessments and grades use multiple measures to assess student progress
There is inter-rater reliability across classrooms
Students are assessed for what they know and are able to demonstrate
Students and families can continually monitor progress using an online grading system

LEVER 4: Student-centered differentiation

		PRINCIPAL ACTIONS
STAGE 1		Articulate a system of **preventions** and **interventions** that include classroom-based practices and strategies that all teachers implement
		Identify the lowest-performing students and create plans to support them
		Allot extra time in the school day for core subjects for all students not yet achieving at grade level (e.g., creating two literacy periods—one to teach at grade level and one to teach developing skills for those not on grade level)
		Dismantle any adult or student beliefs that students who excel will fit a specific gender, race, or socioeconomic profile
STAGE 2		Continue to develop an explicit pyramid of interventions and preventions
		Create process for the development of an individual plan for every student in your school, addressing both preventions and interventions
		Provide students who need additional supports with required interventions
		Ensure that teachers and teacher teams create lessons and units that allow for creativity and original thinking to support all learners
		Lead sessions to develop and implement strengths-based interventions for students who have mastered content
STAGE 3		Identify effective and aligned community resources to increase time and talent dedicated to student interventions (e.g., college student tutors, parent support, resources and space provided by local businesses)
		Build consistency with teachers and teacher teams on how and when to adjust pacing

ACTION 1: Interventions, Preventions, and Accelerations

SCHOOL ACTIONS
Rapid interventions target groups of students who have significant learning gaps and/or who lack key foundational skills
IEPs are clearly written and identify multiple strategies that are closely followed
Students who are in danger of failing a course receive interventions immediately upon first warning sign; services are provided prior to the failure
A student tracking system is in place that uses assessment information, course grades, teacher referrals, and attendance to track each individual student and his or her intensity and schedule of interventions
Students not making progress at the anticipated pace are given extra support in class; differentiation is implemented in every classroom
Teachers consistently differentiate lessons to include parallel experiences for students who have previously learned or mastered content
Students who master content and finish work quickly are not asked to complete additional work repeating the skill
School staff and leaders engage students in the creation and implementation of their interventions
Regular classroom instruction identifies and addresses varied student needs and includes prevention and scaffolding to reduce the need for additional interventions
Students receive rapid, data-driven interventions matched to current needs, and intervention assignments and schedules are frequently updated to reflect student needs and progress
Teachers work with students to modify pacing to ensure that students who master content more quickly are able to accelerate their exploration of a concept
When they have completed required tasks, all students are given opportunities to pursue independent projects based on their individual interests

School Culture

EFFECTIVE SCHOOL CULTURES MAINTAIN HIGH PERFOR-MANCE EXPECTATIONS that nurture students and foster joy in learning; these cultures are positive, productive, and intentional in the desire to integrate academic and social-emotional learning.

The following are the levers that help leaders implement a culture of high expectations:

- Establishing shared school mission, values, and **behaviors** focused on college success for every student

- Building and maintaining meaningful relationships among teachers and staff, focusing on creating a culture where all students are valued

- Purposefully engaging families and communities in the academic and social success of students

Strong school cultures begin with a shared vision and mission that guide the work of adults and students. In many cases, leaders may have a strong initial influence on how the vision and mission are articulated, but for these concepts to truly drive changes in expectations and changes in practice, they must come to be collaboratively developed and owned by stakeholders throughout the school community. To bring the vision and mission to life, leaders and their teams use the vision and mission to define values for their community; they make the values tangible by translating them into behavioral expectations. These expectations are differentiated by grade and hold adults accountable for creating an environment that values all students. Leaders collaborate with the school community to outline and consistently implement rewards for students who demonstrate the values, and consequences when students commit infractions.

> Effective school cultures maintain high performance expectations that nurture students and foster joy in learning; these cultures are positive, productive, and intentional in the desire to find the balance between academic and social-emotional learning.

TRANSFORMATIONAL PRINCIPALS IN ACTION

Lori Phillips

When New Leader Lori Phillips was assigned to be principal of Dunbar Elementary in Memphis, Tennessee, she determined through observations and interviews that to improve academic performance, she had to address the negative culture and the lack of order in the building. Phillips reflected, "Without structure and a positive climate, there is no way you can focus on academics. I knew we'd be able to shift our focus to improving instruction once we had order and a positive learning climate." She established consistent expectations for student and staff behavior across the school and modeled the behavior she wanted to see. These consistent expectations made it clear how infractions were to be addressed. According to Phillips, "Chaotic and unruly behavior in the cafeteria and in the hallways improved right away. Children came in the building quietly and were no longer wild and loud. Teachers quickly learned not to discipline children by sending them out of their classrooms. And there was no running in and out of classrooms as there had been before."

Adults also have the opportunity to create supportive cultures through relationships with students in which they listen to and respect student opinions, voices, and needs. To move toward a culture where adults create meaningful relationships with students, many schools must work on issues of cultural competency and equity to ensure that the adults have high expectations for students regardless of their race, class, or ethnicity.

TRANSFORMATIONAL PRINCIPALS IN ACTION

Jennifer Garcia

New Leader Principal Jennifer Garcia at Aspire Centennial College Preparatory Academy in Los Angeles, California, delivered ongoing professional development based on a book by Angela Valenzuela called *Subtractive Schooling: U.S. Mexican Youth and the Politics of Caring*. Garcia used the case study examined in the book as an entry point to increase self-reflection and cultural competency among staff members. She used the book to expand and explore teachers' perceptions and beliefs while connecting the study to their work in the school.

Schools also need to ensure that families are engaged in meaningful ways that support students' learning and that they are considered key partners in achieving the school's instructional goals by encouraging their children's focus on learning and academic achievement.

Students and adults learn more, work harder, and function better when they are in supportive cultures. Leaders play a pivotal role in setting the tone and establishing the culture in the building.

> **Students and adults learn more, work harder, and function better when they are in supportive cultures. Leaders play a pivotal role in setting the tone and establishing the culture in the building.**

 **Culture Category Map**

Lever 1:
Shared Mission and Values

Schools establish and maintain shared mission, values, and behaviors focused on college success for every student

Actions

- **Vision, Mission, and Values:** Collaborate to create a clear and compelling vision, mission, and set of values
- **Behavioral Expectations:** Translate vision, mission, and values into specific behavioral expectations for adults and students that are described, taught, and consistently implemented
- **Adult and Student Efficacy:** Ensure that adults and students believe in their ability to reach ambitious academic goals through hard work, effective instruction, and feedback
- **Social-Emotional Learning Skills and Supports:** Teach behavioral and social-emotional skills and ensure that supports are in place to guide students' navigation of their academic and personal lives

Lever 2: Relationships

Teachers and staff build and maintain meaningful relationships, focusing on creating a culture where all students are valued

Actions

- **Supportive Adult-Student Relationships:** Build strong relationships with students
- **Cultural Competency and Diversity:** Leverage the strengths of a diverse community to create an equity-focused school community
- **Student Voice:** Create structural opportunities for students to provide input and leadership within the school

Lever 3: Family and Community Engagement

Schools purposefully engage families and communities in the academic and social success of students

Actions

- **Involving Family and Community:** Support student aspirations and success by engaging families and the community

LEVER 1: Shared mission and values

	PRINCIPAL ACTIONS
STAGE 1	Collaborate with aligned staff members to create (or revise) a compelling vision, mission, and set of values focused on college success factors
	Scaffold the communication of the vision, mission, and values in phases that staff can digest
	Create ongoing structures and opportunities for adults and students to reinforce the mission and values
STAGE 2	Establish systems to consistently review and revise the vision, mission, and values with a broad group of stakeholders
	Ensure that the values promote successful **social-emotional skills** that will help students succeed in college
	Explicitly link academic success in school to consistent effort
STAGE 3	Benchmark success against other high-performing schools (conduct visits) to evaluate and refine the vision, mission, and values
	Put systems in place that will maintain a focus on attaining the vision

ACTION 1: Vision, Mission, and Values

SCHOOL ACTIONS
The leadership team and/or a small group of leaders demonstrate alignment to and support for the school mission, vision, and values
The vision, mission, and values are informed by students and staff
The values include some variant of:
• Every student can and will be ready to succeed in college
• Consistent effort—not innate ability—leads to success
• Adults and students share ownership for student success
School staff members share a common understanding of vision, mission, and values in practice; can describe the vision and the mission; and can explain how they are present in the daily life of the school
The leadership team translates the vision and mission of the school into a step-by-step school improvement plan
The leadership team owns the communication and modeling of the vision, mission, and values of the school
Stakeholders are deeply involved in the process of refinement and revision of the vision, mission, and values
Staff rely on vision, mission, and values for all major decisions and planning
Students have internalized the school's vision and mission
Students drive school direction in alignment with the school vision and mission

LEVER 1: Shared mission and values

	PRINCIPAL ACTIONS
STAGE 1	Describe how staff and students can enact the mission and values through specific behaviors
	Articulate and model the importance of social-emotional and social responsibility skills and their connections to student success in school, college, and life
	Build a school-level system of rewards and consequences that result from specific behaviors
	Create an accountability system so that all infractions are addressed in a consistent manner, and hold staff responsible for consistently implementing rewards and consequences with all students, not only those they directly teach
	Ensure that adults know how behavioral expectations translate to all parts of the school day, including opening of day, lunchtime, class transitions
STAGE 2	Establish age- and developmentally appropriate behavioral expectations
	Create structures to implement frequent teaching and reteaching of behaviors
	Expose staff continually to grade- and age-appropriate behaviors and supports
	Use multiple forms of student data—including disaggregated discipline data, attendance, participation in activities, and who is publicly celebrated—to monitor and measure adoption of behaviors
	Create structures and opportunities for students to teach other students and serve as role models
	Develop the school's capacity to respond to students' behavioral and social-emotional needs in developmentally appropriate ways
STAGE 3	Build student capacity and experience in teaching the values and behaviors to others and for holding one another accountable for living them
	Implement structures for peer mediation where students serve as the role models for one another

ACTION 2: Behavioral Expectations

SCHOOL ACTIONS
There are multiple formal structures through which school values and expected behaviors are taught and reinforced—daily rewards and consequences are published and shared widely
Student social-emotional and social responsibility skills are included and explicitly named in the expectations of behavior
All members of the school community use common language to describe the school values, and share a common understanding of expected behaviors
Rituals and public forums celebrate staff and students who model expectations and demonstrate behaviors that reflect the values
All staff teach and reinforce behavioral expectations while implementing the system of rewards and consequences
Induction systems are in place for new and returning staff, students, families, and communities
Adults use teachable moments and find time to reinforce and teach behaviors
Students who live the behaviors are given additional freedoms and demonstrate high levels of personal responsibility in social and academic settings
Staff consistently implement the discipline system and reinforce the established behavioral expectations
Social responsibility skills (service to others) are taught to all students
Systems are in place to review the number of office referrals and analyze them to identify patterns or trends in referral data
Disaggregated referral data is regularly reviewed to ensure that consequences are not meted out differently based on race, class, or ethnicity
Students have a clear and consistent role in teaching behaviors to new and younger students
Students energize their peers and focus on achievement
Students hold one another accountable for living by the expectations for student behavior
Students mediate moments of conflict within the school

LEVER 1: Shared mission and values

	PRINCIPAL ACTIONS
STAGE 1	Create opportunities for students and staff to observe schools where similar populations of students are succeeding
	Teach adults how to support and teach effective-effort strategies
	Shape the environment to make explicit links between student aspirations, effort, and achievement (e.g., publicly displayed school symbols and rituals)
	Model and create a system through which staff and students develop and track short- and long-term goals
	Provide opportunities for adults to receive feedback and track their improvement
STAGE 2	Create conditions where students are able to take intellectual risks, make mistakes, and analyze the impact of their actions
	Create college and career access experiences for all students
	Set expectations that all teachers will develop **mastery experiences** for their students to build student **efficacy**
STAGE 3	Celebrate staff and students who persist in the face of challenges and adversity

ACTION 3: Adult and Student Efficacy

SCHOOL ACTIONS
Clear messages about effort leading to near- and long-term success are visible and vocalized by all
College and career aspirations are a visible part of students' everyday experience in the school
All students engage in a college-going–career development process that includes setting short- and long-term learning goals and college and career goals
Students have opportunities to experience mastery in multiple settings to reinforce their sense that they can achieve
Students have multiple opportunities to make decisions about their learning experiences
Students develop short- and long-term goals, and strategies for how they will attain their goals
Students value feedback and view it as an integral part of their learning
Students engage in rich college-going and career access experiences
(High school) Dedicated staff are in place to help students understand the college admissions process (research colleges, apply to college, and apply for financial aid and scholarships)
Students energize their peers by making public their progress toward goals
Students do not give up when faced with adversity
Students see challenges as part of the learning process and seek help when they need it

LEVER 1: Shared mission and values

	PRINCIPAL ACTIONS
STAGE 1	Ensure that all teachers have some training and support in teaching social-emotional skills
	Create a pyramid of behavioral interventions that mirrors the academic intervention pyramid with social-emotional development support
	Design and implement systems to gather positive and negative school culture and behavior data
	Establish a basic system of identifying the students who need more interventions or additional supports
	Create a student intervention team to support students in crisis
STAGE 2	Create a highly effective and efficient pyramid of interventions and additional supports (including wraparound services for the students with the most significant needs) and ensure that proactive mental health support is provided to students in need of additional supports
	Lead conversations with staff about social-emotional development and about diffusing challenging situations
	Ensure that all adults are trained to identify and support students in need of non-classroom-based supports
	Monitor data to ensure that no child is invisible and that every student has access to supports within and beyond the school
STAGE 3	Weave social-emotional learning and personal development into the academic program so that students, staff, and families recognize how these skills support academic achievement
	Ensure that interventions support academic, social, and emotional needs for all students

ACTION 4: Social-Emotional Learning Skills and Supports

SCHOOL ACTIONS
Teachers encourage all students to name their emotions and to find appropriate ways to manage stress and pressure
Students practice describing their emotions and managing their behavior even when upset
Data systems exist to track all discipline referrals and interventions
Data is used to identify structural issues that need to be addressed (e.g., transitions that consistently cause problems, times of day that are problems for students)
Teacher team structures exist to identify students with significant behavioral and learning challenges
Students demonstrate empathy toward others, resist negative social pressure, make ethical decisions, and exhibit respect
Crisis intervention teams train all adults to learn how to support students in crisis
Students in crisis are referred and receive their first intervention within forty-eight hours
All staff receive professional development on how to implement the social-emotional and career skills curriculum
Students can analyze how thoughts and emotions affect their decision making and behavior and can use that knowledge to make informed choices
Students who are at risk are identified prior to incident and receive additional supports
Multiple members of the staff have the skills to serve on the crisis intervention team
Students implement strategies to work in teams, manage time and projects, and make responsible decisions

SCHOOL CULTURE   LEVER 1

LEVER 2: Relationships

SCHOOL CULTURE

	PRINCIPAL ACTIONS
STAGE 1	Create time, structures, and processes for adults to build strong relationships with students
	Design a plan for every student to have at least one one-to-one caring adult relationship in the building
	Create structures to facilitate adults' developing the skills to provide authentic care for students
STAGE 2	Create teacher team structures that look at the whole student, not just his or her results in a particular content area
	Organize the student community into cohorts with supporting rituals and routines that build positive cohort identity and foster strong relationships among and between students and adults
STAGE 3	Create times and structures for adults across content areas to discuss students' performance and behavior in multiple settings
	Provide space for adults to talk about the social-emotional needs of students
	Facilitate cohort and grade relationships among students to support student learning

ACTION 1: Supportive Adult-Student Relationships

SCHOOL ACTIONS
Students all have at least one adult who checks in with them regularly to provide support and who knows all aspects of their academic and behavioral progress to date
Staff members have a profile for every one of their students that includes the student's strength and growth areas
(High school) Staff and students meet on a regular daily or weekly basis to explore academic and nonacademic topics
Adults take responsibility to proactively support each student's overall academic and social success
All staff feel comfortable reinforcing behavioral expectations and supporting students and school spaces, beyond their own classrooms
All students are known well by multiple adults
Adults meet frequently to identify individual student needs and work together to support and monitor individual student progress, behavior, and social-emotional development
Staff lead culture-building activities with students and with parents and families

LEVER 2: Relationships

	PRINCIPAL ACTIONS
STAGE 1	Share a focus on bringing equitable practices to the school community and hold **cultural competence** to be an important part of the school's culture
	Provide formal and informal professional development to teachers and staff to improve their understanding of how their own worldviews inform their interpretations of the world
	Create opportunities for staff to learn about and experience the community surrounding the school
	Address and correct moments of cultural incompetence and challenge
STAGE 2	Lead conversations with staff about inequities and about honoring diversity
	Lead teachers through a process to identify students' strengths and assets
STAGE 3	Build staff capacity to lead and create culture-building activities
	Mobilize and galvanize the community to interrupt social inequities in the school and beyond

ACTION 2: Cultural Competency and Diversity

Teachers seek to understand how other individuals (adults and students) experience the world while not making assumptions about them based on visible characteristics

Data is disaggregated, and existing systems and structures are reviewed to ensure that traditionally underserved and underperforming students are not being treated unfairly

The school community values and promotes the cultural values of students and parents

Staff take responsibility for knowing each student's cultural background, assets, and growth areas

Pedagogy is culturally and developmentally responsive and relevant

Teachers use culturally competent language and demonstrate knowledge of students' development

Staff consistently interrupt systems and structures that promote inequity within the school

LEVER 2: Relationships

	PRINCIPAL ACTIONS
STAGE 1	Create systems and processes to gather student input and to build opportunities for student voice
STAGE 2	Create structures and developmental opportunities for children to show leadership voice (e.g., student council, student peer review board) Build the capacity for staff to support student leadership
STAGE 3	Create opportunities for students of all ages to manage projects and make decisions

ACTION 3: Student Voice

SCHOOL ACTIONS
Students have opportunities to contribute ideas for school improvement
Students use their voice to express their feelings and ideas in ways that are appropriate in the school settings
Students know how to respectfully challenge adults and others in a way that allows their voices to be heard
Students are frequently recognized for their contributions to the school community
Students have multiple opportunities to contribute to school practices and decision making about their learning experiences
Students identify and challenge injustices within the school and in the community (e.g., advocating on behalf of others)
Students are invited to express their feelings and ideas about how to improve their experiences in school and to attain their goals
Students analyze data to inform and lead change
Students take a systems approach to address injustices in the school and in the larger community

LEVER 3: Family and community engagement

	PRINCIPAL ACTIONS
STAGE 1	Create a flexible engagement strategy that values multiple types of family and community interactions
	Develop and implement short- and long-term plans for family and community engagement tailored to the school and community context
	Identify two or three schoolwide practices to engage families based on analysis of the community's need
STAGE 2	Train the staff on how to engage with families and community members respectfully and effectively
	Create multiple opportunities for engagement to ensure that interactions do not feel hierarchical to families or community members
	Track and analyze whether all families are engaging in positive two-way exchanges
STAGE 3	Gather and evaluate data from families and community members about the quality of engagement
	Provide ongoing and relevant trainings and supports for community members and families to support and foster high levels of engagement

ACTION 1: Involving Family and Community

SCHOOL ACTIONS
The leadership team builds awareness of biases about what family is and what family engagement means
At least one person, in addition to the principal, is designated as a lead in family and community engagement work
Systems are in place that communicate with families on a daily, weekly, and monthly basis about their child's performance (both positive and negative)
Families are actively involved in key moments of student learning
Multiple communication strategies with families are integrated into teacher roles and responsibilities
Family and community engagement data is reviewed regularly, and plans are adapted as needed
Families are viewed by all faculty and staff as critical partners in each student's academic and personal development
Staff members take collective responsibility to engage families and the community

Talent Management

THE TALENT MANAGEMENT CATEGORY DESCRIBES THE ACTIONS and practices needed to develop and support effective teachers and staff members. Effective staff members are necessary to enact the vision and mission and the instructional strategies outlined in the Learning and Teaching and Culture categories. The relationships among these categories require leaders to consider the ways in which they can move actions in all of these categories forward in concert.

Our experience shows that the most effective principals are those who know how to develop their staff and strategically distribute instructional leadership; they delegate authority to teacher leaders who are able to build a culture of high expectations, analyze data to understand students' strengths and needs, and design and correct instruction so that students meet their learning objectives.

School leaders align the teachers and staff in their building through several key activities:

- Recruiting, selecting, assigning, and onboarding staff

- Developing a well-aligned school team comprising an instructional leadership team and teacher leaders who support effective instructional practices

- Monitoring and managing individual staff performance

- Establishing professional learning structures to drive instructional improvement

Recruitment and hiring are key moments when leaders can assess potential staff members for their belief in and alignment to the vision, their content knowledge, and their instructional strengths. To ensure that they found the right team members, many of the leaders we visited began their recruitment and hiring processes in midwinter.

TRANSFORMATIONAL PRINCIPALS IN ACTION

Eric Westendorf

One of the highest priorities for the leadership team at E. L. Haynes Public Charter School, in Washington, D.C., was recruiting and hiring the right faculty. As New Leader Eric Westendorf, the school's chief academic officer, pointed out, "We know that when we get it right, it makes a big difference for kids, and when we get it wrong, it takes up a lot of time trying to address the problem." The E. L. Haynes leadership team began their recruitment and hiring cycle each January with a meeting to assess their staffing needs and review the effectiveness of the previous year's recruitment and hiring practices. On the basis of this assessment, the team set priorities and revised or refined their processes and tools as needed.

Further, leaders and their teams focus on assessing the quality of the candidates who are applying for roles.

TRANSFORMATIONAL PRINCIPALS IN ACTION

Tina Chekan

Principal Tina Chekan of Propel McKeesport Charter School in McKeesport, Pennsylvania, employed an extensive array of rubrics and activities to assess potential hires for teaching positions. At each stage, multiple staff members assessed candidates using rubrics and scoring sheets to determine if they had the desired combination of pedagogical skills and commitment to student academic success. Chekan made the final decision as to who would be hired. She explained, "Our goal is to be the highest-achieving high-poverty school in the region. That is a goal in our Staff Success Statement, which we discuss at every staff meeting and training. But not every educator truly believes that all kids can achieve no matter their circumstances in life. We need teachers who have a 'no excuses' philosophy. They must have a strong work ethic and be willing to put forth extra hours for professional development… To find those teachers, we need more than a standard fifteen-minute interview. We need to assess the candidates on multiple dimensions."

Effective leaders also know they cannot move the school without other leaders in the building, so they create opportunities for others to assume leadership roles.

TRANSFORMATIONAL PRINCIPALS IN ACTION

Grace Reid

At Barnard Elementary School in Washington, D.C., Principal Grace Reid gave teachers leading roles in staff development. She encouraged teacher-led presentations during staff development time. She also asked veteran teachers to mentor new teachers and set goals for their development. Reid said that the mentoring relationship provided new teachers with support as they became acclimated, and fostered collaboration among all teachers. It also provided opportunities for veteran teachers to practice and build their instructional and leadership skills.

Once the instructional leadership team has been established, leaders work to provide frequent actionable feedback to teachers and staff members as part of their ongoing performance management work. As part of this performance management process, leaders set clear expectations for quality work with all staff members and help staff members develop a shared understanding of how their work can support the schoolwide goals. On the basis of the established expectations, staff members work with school leaders to identify specific areas to improve their individual practice.

> As part of this performance management process, leaders set clear expectations for quality work with all staff members and help staff members develop a shared understanding of how their work can support the schoolwide goals.

TRANSFORMATIONAL PRINCIPALS IN ACTION

Mark DiBella

The teacher evaluation process at YES Prep North Central in Houston, Texas, where Mark DiBella served as school director, included a formal midyear evaluation in addition to an end-of-year summative evaluation. DiBella said, "The purpose of our midyear evaluation is to ensure that we're getting a chance to focus in on student achievement data and make sure that there is a connection [to] the goals that teachers are setting instructionally … It's a way to make sure that we're having focused conversations around those two things." The midyear evaluation cycle included an announced, full-lesson observation conducted by the dean of instruction to measure each teacher's performance on aspects of the school's Instructional Excellence Rubric. Midyear observation data was cross-checked with the data collected during the fifteen- to twenty-minute observations conducted throughout the first semester. The midyear observation was followed by a postobservation conference with each teacher to review his or her midyear evaluation, identify target areas for growth, and brainstorm possible second-semester goals in preparation for the year-end summative evaluation meeting.

As an essential part of performance management, staff are also matched with professional learning opportunities that support and facilitate development; these learning moments tie directly to the day-to-day work of the team and include content and approaches that are immediately applicable.

As an essential part of performance management, staff are also matched with professional learning opportunities that support and facilitate development; these learning moments tie directly to the day-to-day work of the team and include content and approaches that are immediately applicable.

Talent Management Category Map

Lever 1: Recruitment and Onboarding

Schools recruit, select, assign, and onboard staff efficiently and effectively

Actions

- **Recruitment:** Identify effective and aligned staff candidates
- **Selection and Hiring:** Implement rigorous screening and hiring procedures
- **Staff Assignment:** Implement processes for strategic staff assignment
- **Induction:** Develop systems to introduce new staff to school expectations, processes, and procedures

Lever 2: Instructional Leadership Team

Schools develop a well-aligned team comprising an instructional leadership team and teacher leaders who support effective instructional practices

Actions

- **Instructional Leadership Team Roles, Expectations, and Supports:** Identify, develop, and support instructional leadership team members
- **Teacher Leadership:** Create ongoing opportunities for teachers to build leadership capacity

Lever 3: Performance Monitoring and Evaluation

School leaders monitor and manage individual staff performance

Actions

- **Performance Expectations:** Set expectations for all staff members that define what standards and actions will be assessed
- **Observation and Actionable Feedback:** Gather evidence of practice through frequent observations and provide concrete feedback
- **Monitoring Implementation:** Assess where changes in practice are occurring and where additional supports are needed
- **Performance Evaluation:** At the end of the year, review all evidence to assess individual performance

Lever 4: Professional Learning and Collaboration

Schools establish professional learning structures that drive instructional improvement

Actions

- **Ongoing Professional Learning:** Provide job-embedded opportunities to learn and practice new skills
- **Collaborative Teacher Team Structures:** Establish structures that facilitate collaborative teacher planning and learning

LEVER 1: Recruitment and onboarding

	PRINCIPAL ACTIONS
STAGE 1	Assess and expand recruiting sources beyond the traditional district candidate pool by reaching out to partner programs, universities, and other available venues
	Hire as early as possible when vacancies are known
	Develop materials that present the school as an attractive place to work
STAGE 2	Recruit for diverse expertise: build networks with traditional and nontraditional teacher sources by reaching out to local universities, partnering with human resources, and asking teachers to tap into their networks
	Engage leadership team members in networking to potential staff members at every opportunity
STAGE 3	Identify vacancies early by working with the leadership team to identify staff who are likely to transition
	Partner with the central HR team to identify talent for hard-to-fill vacancies

LEVER 1

TALENT MANAGEMENT

ACTION 1: **Recruitment**

SCHOOL ACTIONS
Recruitment efforts cast a wide net for candidates outside of traditional venues
The school maintains an ongoing, active recruitment network outside of standard district resources Leadership team members identify many sources for high-quality recruits School branding materials and website are easily accessible and inspire the right staff to apply by sharing key messages about the vision and mission of the school and its hiring processes
Teachers routinely attend hiring fairs and events and tap their own networks to recruit staff

LEVER 1

TALENT MANAGEMENT

LEVER 1: Recruitment and onboarding

	PRINCIPAL ACTIONS
STAGE 1	Develop clear selection criteria and a clear process for selection, including how all decisions will be made
	Select teachers who have demonstrated content knowledge, who share a belief in the potential of all students, and who are willing to learn and develop
	Implement application and interview protocols to rigorously screen prospective teachers for belief that all students can reach college and for commitment to student learning, not just to teaching their content area
STAGE 2	Include demo lessons and formal interviews with teachers, families, and students (where appropriate) as part of the staff selection process
	Organize ongoing professional development for all staff involved in hiring teachers, in order to develop a common vision of the skills and behaviors of a strong candidate
	Develop leadership team members' capacity to manage the selection process
STAGE 3	Set expectations with leadership team members for how responsibilities will be divided, and task them to lead the hiring and selection process

ACTION 2: Selection and Hiring

SCHOOL ACTIONS
Clear selection criteria, protocols, and hiring and induction processes are in place An appropriate number of staff members are certified according to state and district guidelines, including for ELL and special education services
Multiple staff members are involved in multiple aspects of the hiring and selection process and are part of the hiring team Selected candidates demonstrate a willingness to explore and deepen their understandings of students' cultures
The selection process is managed by the leadership team and includes the input of the other key stakeholders (e.g., students, family members, and other members of the community) Multiple stakeholders, including students and community members, have the opportunity to participate in the hiring process

LEVER 1

TALENT MANAGEMENT

LEVER 1: Recruitment and onboarding

	PRINCIPAL ACTIONS
STAGE 1	Assess staff skills and place teachers in grade levels and content areas on the basis of their skills, qualifications, and demonstrated effectiveness
STAGE 2	Identify, from within the current staff, effective teachers who have demonstrated high leadership potential, and recruit them to grade-level and department leadership Balance grade and content teams to ensure that more experienced and effective teachers are mentoring and supporting less experienced teachers
STAGE 3	Assess needs and strategically deploy people based on skill and need, even if that means moving teachers from grades they have taught in the past Formally leverage the strongest teachers to build the capacity of others Develop contingency plans for open positions that include providing additional supports to remaining teachers and strategies to support long-term substitutes

ACTION 3: **Staff Assignment**

SCHOOL ACTIONS
Strengths, not tenure or other considerations, are used to determine teacher placement
Strongest teachers are placed with lowest-performing students and in grades that have proven to have long-term impact on student success and retention
Grade-level and content-area teams have strong leadership
Teams comprise staff with a mix of experience, strengths, and tenure at the school
Highly effective teachers are asked to formally develop and support teachers on their teams who are not as strong
Long-term substitutes or staff who are taking on additional responsibilities to provide coverage when there is a vacancy are supported while being held to high standards

LEVER 1

TALENT MANAGEMENT

LEVER 1: Recruitment and onboarding

	PRINCIPAL ACTIONS
STAGE 1	Create induction processes for new staff at the time of placement in order to share expectations, cultural norms of the school, processes, and procedures
STAGE 2	At the start of every school year, lead returning staff through some parts of the induction process to remind them of the school's key goals and expectations for improving student achievement Partner with the leadership team to plan and revise induction activities based on their effectiveness in past years
STAGE 3	Assess the impact of induction activities to improve on the induction process and to ensure that induction has a positive effect on staff performance and feeling about the school

ACTION 4: Induction

School has intensive induction and mentoring processes for any new staff

The induction system is ongoing and touches all staff throughout the school year to maintain a common vision for the school

Induction activities are viewed as positive culture-building moments

Multiple staff members have a role in leading induction activities for new and returning staff

Interim staff members participate in a modified induction process to ensure that all adults share similar expectations

LEVER 1

TALENT MANAGEMENT

LEVER 2: Instructional leadership team

	PRINCIPAL ACTIONS
STAGE 1	Define the roles and responsibilities for the instructional leadership team: supporting and leading teacher team meetings, leading **data-driven instruction** cycles, conducting teacher observations, providing feedback, and completing final evaluations
	Assess the alignment of the current instructional leadership team members to the school's vision, mission, approach to instruction, and culture, and take immediate steps to remove or replace any members who are unwilling or unable to carry out the current expectations
	Model effective team meeting protocols and processes for looking at student outcomes and planning responsive strategies
	Create monitoring systems to track the work of instructional leadership team members and their teams, looking at consistency and quality of implementation
	Ensure that the processes and roles of the instructional leadership team are clear to all members of the staff
STAGE 2	Design yearlong professional learning for the instructional leadership team members to build consistency in their assessment of teacher practice
	Build capacity of instructional leadership team members to conduct observations and provide effective feedback
	Develop reporting systems so that instructional leadership team members can share feedback, input, and concerns of the teams they are leading
	Create clarity around decision making, especially letting staff know when a decision will be yours or made by consensus
	Develop a succession plan for essential roles on the instructional leadership team
STAGE 3	Build systems for distributed leadership through which members of the instructional leadership team manage specific initiatives and grade-level teams or departments
	Expand the roles of the instructional leadership team to include teacher evaluation (when policy allows)
	Provide instructional leadership team members opportunities for additional autonomy to manage projects and teams

ACTION 1: Instructional Leadership Team Roles, Expectations, and Supports

SCHOOL ACTIONS
Instructional leadership team roles and responsibilities are clear and transparent
Identified instructional leadership team members have an individualized development plan based on their strength and growth areas
Instructional leadership team members take part in regular learning walks during which they are looking for the implementation of specific practices
Instructional leadership team meetings focus on student work and formative data
Staff understand the roles and responsibilities of the instructional leadership team
The instructional leadership team consistently models and enforces schoolwide philosophy, core values, responsibility, and efficacy
Instructional leadership team members conduct observations and provide effective coaching and feedback
Instructional leadership team members have clear and consistent ways in which to share the concerns, challenges, and successes of the teams they are leading
Instructional leadership team members use consistent protocols and processes to lead their departmental or grade-level teams
Instructional leadership is provided by multiple instructional leadership team members using consistent protocols and processes and a relentless focus on data
Instructional leadership team members successfully lead autonomous projects

LEVER 2: Instructional leadership team

	PRINCIPAL ACTIONS
STAGE 1	Name and describe career pathways that teachers and noninstructional staff can pursue in their current roles, and more broadly within the school and the district
	Provide leadership opportunities and support for leadership roles for highly skilled staff who demonstrate a commitment to the school vision and priorities
	Utilize effective teachers who share values, beliefs, and commitment for key positions on the instructional leadership team
STAGE 2	Identify midlevel and high-performing teachers for development and leadership opportunities
	Track retention rates of effective teachers to identify trends and patterns
	Inspire effective teachers to stay in their roles by providing positive feedback for high-quality work and selecting them for school-level leadership opportunities
STAGE 3	Encourage teachers to participate in high-quality self-reflection and action research activities (e.g., National Board certification, advanced degree programs) that continue to build their expertise

LEVER 2

TALENT MANAGEMENT

ACTION 1: Teacher Leadership

SCHOOL ACTIONS
Teachers begin to participate in regular development opportunities to build their leadership capacity
Teachers begin to facilitate professional development for others to gain leadership experience
Aligned and skilled teachers are identified and developed as leaders in their classrooms, in their grade-level teams, or on the instructional leadership team
Teachers are encouraged to create new leadership opportunities if they see a gap or an area for development
All teachers have opportunities to stretch their leadership skills with supports and parameters appropriate to their current level of expertise
High-performing teachers are given multiple opportunities to develop and demonstrate their own leadership
Teachers regularly design and lead professional learning activities as part of their leadership development
Staff members proactively assume leadership roles
To the greatest extent possible, retention of teachers and recommendations for leadership are determined on the basis of demonstrated effectiveness as measured by student learning
Highest-skilled and fully aligned teachers receive substantial leadership opportunities and are supported in taking on these roles (even to the point of leaving the school to become leaders in other schools if necessary for their continued development)
Structures are in place to support teacher retention by creating opportunities for growth and development

LEVER 2

TALENT MANAGEMENT

LEVER 3: Performance monitoring and evaluation

	PRINCIPAL ACTIONS
STAGE 1	Set and share performance expectations aligned to schoolwide goals and school priorities for each staff member
	Ensure that each staff member is aware of the standards and metrics against which his or her performance will be assessed
	Build shared understanding of any required evaluation systems by exploring the concepts and rubrics at the school level
	Explain all components of the performance management cycle, including individual goal and target setting, formal observations, midyear reviews, and final summative evaluations
STAGE 2	Differentiate targets for each grade and subject area based on historical performance data for that grade as well as for the incoming cohort of students
STAGE 3	Individualize the performance management system for each staff member, including • Individual student achievement targets • Individual performance goals • System for consistent monitoring and follow-up on improvement

ACTION 1: Performance Expectations

Performance expectations are clear, and they match the job responsibilities and design

The performance management schedule, calendar, and sequence are transparent

The performance management system includes team and individual goals for each staff member that align to the schoolwide goals and priorities

Every adult in the school is aligned to high achievement goals and understands his or her specific role

LEVER 3

TALENT MANAGEMENT

LEVER 3: Performance monitoring and evaluation

	PRINCIPAL ACTIONS
STAGE 1	Create an observation protocol for walkthroughs, which are done frequently with schoolwide foci
	Find creative ways (sticky notes, email) to give frequent feedback on progress with nonnegotiable instructional practices; include discussions of specific student work and data
STAGE 2	Create systems and schedules for conducting frequent, brief, and differentiated observations by members of the instructional leadership team on the basis of teacher need
	Provide regular feedback and/or have systems in place so that staff receive feedback from a member of the instructional leadership team
	Use analyses of student learning outcomes to update observation protocols
STAGE 3	Expand observation protocol and practice to include consistent schoolwide expectations, individual teacher development areas, and study of specific student subgroups as identified by data
	Implement a system for offering consistent support and follow-up to gauge improvement that includes formal and informal feedback from members of the leadership team, master teachers, and other school leaders
	Feedback is based on school goals, schoolwide nonnegotiable goals, and teacher-generated goals

ACTION 2: Observation and Actionable Feedback

SCHOOL ACTIONS
The instructional leadership team begins conducting staff observations
Teachers receive concrete and actionable feedback within forty-eight hours of an observation or walkthrough
All staff are observed, at least briefly, on a weekly basis, with a focus on schoolwide consistent routines and schoolwide priorities for improvement
Every classroom is visited for five to ten minutes at least two to three times per week as part of ongoing learning walks
An expanded group of school leaders engage in observations and provide feedback based on a consistent protocol and set of expectations
Instructional leaders review lesson plans for evidence of reteaching and spiraling
Instructional leadership team members provide frequent observations and feedback to staff on instructional practices and handling of student conduct concerns, with follow-up to ensure improvement
The observation protocol and practice include consistent schoolwide expectations, individual teacher development areas, and study of specific student subgroups as identified by data
All new teachers and teachers with specific development needs are mentored by highly skilled peers
Peers are able to provide ongoing feedback to one another on learning walks and interclassroom visits

LEVER 3

TALENT MANAGEMENT

LEVER 3: Performance monitoring and evaluation

		PRINCIPAL ACTIONS
STAGE 1		Ensure consistent implementation of nonnegotiable instructional strategies by comparing lesson plans to what is occurring in classrooms
		Become a constant presence in the classrooms of staff identified as "not aligned and/or unskilled and unwilling/unable to develop" and develop a plan to counsel out or remove them through existing formal processes
		Once expectations are established, conduct a staff inventory that determines staff member skill (certifications, tenure, commendations) and will to improve as well as any disciplinary actions
		Conduct a series of preliminary observations and conversations with each staff member to assess his or her strengths and weaknesses to determine the most effective supports
STAGE 2		Hold teachers accountable for student learning, including displaying student work during classroom observations and referencing student data during teacher debriefs
		Support struggling teachers with specific improvement plans that focus on what steps they will take to improve their performance
		Prioritize support for teachers with clear development needs, including full lesson observations and peer mentoring
		Use teacher assessment data and student performance data to determine teacher development activities
		Assign instructional leadership team members to work with specific sets of teachers on the basis of their skills and areas of growth
STAGE 3		Track and monitor staff review data to ensure that monitoring is occurring and that individual staff interventions are effective

ACTION 3: Monitoring Implementation

SCHOOL ACTIONS
Nonaligned or poorly performing staff are closely monitored through additional reviews of work and observations Staff who are identified as less skilled are provided with ongoing support and are prioritized for more frequent observation Nonaligned staff are identified, and if they do not make improvements, they are counseled out or, where necessary, removed through existing formal processes
Leadership team members monitor teachers through observations and through review of data and student work Struggling staff are put on specific performance improvement plans that address their specific needs Each teacher is involved in differentiated support activities that match his or her areas of growth
Staff demonstrate consistent high-quality practices for instruction and student and staff culture Developing staff are taking rapid action to close the gap between current practice and expectations for quality practice

LEVER 3: Performance monitoring and evaluation

PRINCIPAL ACTIONS
STAGE 1 — Compile multiple data sources to assess teacher practice Have a second reviewer analyze evidence for any teacher approaching tenure
STAGE 2 — Model, for leadership team members allowed to participate in evaluation, how to assess multiple data points to come to a practice rating that is based on evidence rather than judgments Identify and move out the consistently ineffective teachers
STAGE 3 — Use effective processes for managing underperforming staff, including learning specific district-approved practices for HR management (e.g., specific union regulations and timelines)

ACTION 4: **Performance Evaluation**

SCHOOL ACTIONS
A performance management system is in place, and end-of-year ratings are based on documented evidence from multiple sources Tenure decisions are reviewed to ensure that the teacher meets expectations for teaching skill, beliefs, and willingness to learn and develop
Staff have ongoing conversations with members of the leadership team about their performance Underperforming staff are put on improvement plans with appropriate supports Staff who are voluntarily transitioning from the school are invited to participate in an exit interview to improve retention
Summative evaluation is seen as a cumulative moment of feedback—rather than a snapshot—because staff receive frequent feedback about their performance and, as needed, are given ample notice and opportunity to improve

LEVER 4: Professional learning and collaboration

	PRINCIPAL ACTIONS
STAGE 1	Design a comprehensive professional learning plan and calendar aligned to school goals and trends observed in learning walks
	Directly engage in development sessions as leader/facilitator or active participant; set clear expectations for implementation of presented practices and strategies, and monitor their implementation and use
	Identify classrooms and schools that demonstrate strong instructional programs and results; target them for staff visits and reflection
STAGE 2	Develop a clear plan for adult learning across the school that aligns areas for whole-school improvement, teacher team areas of focus, and individual development priorities
	Create structures for job-embedded collaborative learning: professional learning communities, protected time for grade-level and content-area planning, and protocols for systematic examination of practice
STAGE 3	Structure professional learning around compelling student data
	Provide individual teachers and teacher teams access to new research and other developmental resources geared to identified development needs
	Create individual development plans and focus areas for each teacher

ACTION 1: Ongoing Professional Learning

SCHOOL ACTIONS
The school has a clear professional learning calendar of topics aligned to established school expectations
Professional development for all staff focuses on schoolwide instructional nonnegotiable goals; aligned, rigorous curriculum mapping; and consistent implementation of instructional strategies
The professional learning plan includes cycles of lesson observations, large-group training sessions, teacher team meetings, and coaching/mentoring for individual staff
Teachers participate in regular development opportunities that seek to build their capacity
Teacher-driven professional development focuses on student learning challenges and progress toward student achievement goals; it occurs during the school day and includes teacher team meetings and peer visits
All new teachers and all teachers with specific development needs are mentored by highly skilled peers
Professional development is job embedded and directly relates to the school's goals, occurs during the school day, and supports quick improvements in practice
Staff share a collective awareness of individual skills and growth areas; they self-direct professional development based on student achievement outcomes

LEVER 4

TALENT MANAGEMENT

LEVER 4: Professional learning and collaboration

	PRINCIPAL ACTIONS
STAGE 1	Create teacher teams (if not already in place) and protocols focused on student outcomes, student data, and student work
	Articulate clear expectations for common planning time; model the process and the unwavering focus on student learning
STAGE 2	Implement protocols in team meetings for frequent group analysis of data, in pursuit of root causes
	Observe teacher team meetings and provide feedback on their processes to help them develop as a team
STAGE 3	Provide individual teachers and teacher teams access to new research and other developmental resources geared to identified development needs

ACTION 2: Collaborative Teacher Team Structures

Instructional strategies, instructional consistency, instructional development of staff, and definitions of rigor are discussed at teacher team meetings

Teacher teams use protocols and processes designed to guide collaboration

Grade-level and/or content-area teams have common weekly planning times with clear outcomes focused on student learning and not just student behaviors

Teacher teams build common assessments

Intervention teachers collaborate closely with all other classroom teachers to ensure effective planning and instruction to implement IEPs

Instructional leadership team members lead effective teacher team meetings focused on student learning data and student work

Time to review individual student learning data is built into the schedule of collaborative team meetings

Instructional leadership team members serve as instructional leaders in the school, leading effective teacher team meetings focused on student learning data and student work

Teacher team discussions are clearly focused on individual student learning progress and student work, not just general standards and strategies

It is common practice for teams to share best practices and problem-solve together, and teams leverage the individual differences and strengths of each member of the team

LEVER 4

TALENT MANAGEMENT

Operations and Planning

THE OPERATIONS AND PLANNING CATEGORY DESCRIBES THE critical, but often invisible, components of school success and improvement; these components provide staff members the tools, processes, and resources necessary to achieve schoolwide goals.

The Operations and Planning category comprises the following levers:

- Tracking of clear and focused school goals, and adjusting strategy based on progress

- Aligning use of time to make progress toward and attain schoolwide goals

- Aligning budget, external partnerships, and facilities to the strategic plan

- Managing district context and school system relations to ensure a focus on learning

The first lever in the Operations and Planning category focuses on identifying clear goals and measures to guide school improvement and creating action plans and the right structures to implement these plans.

> At East High School in Denver, Principal Youngquist and his team set a schoolwide goal of increasing the number of freshmen attaining the required number of credits to graduate on time from 74 percent to 90 percent. Says Youngquist,
>
> > One of the keys for me to be sure that this program is effective is to constantly keep our minds on the ultimate goal. So we have yet to achieve that 90 percent on track, but that is the goal I present to teachers at every meeting... I want to make sure that people understand we have a very high goal that we're driving toward, and this is a strategy that we believe will take us there, but we want to check it and make sure that this is heading us toward the right direction. I also want to make sure that people understand that we'll be responsive to data that says that we're not headed the right direction.

Once teams identify shared goals, they need to ensure that time is well planned and maximized to support the achievement of those goals. In addition to focusing time on student learning, these efforts help staff members feel that their time and work are being respected and supported by the school leadership.

The focus on time extends to ensuring that there is a master schedule and a consistent calendar shared across the community. The schedule creates consistent blocks of time for teacher team meetings, interventions, professional learning, and community events. Once set, the schedule is public and times are honored so that the team understands how the school day will be structured and can plan against the schedule.

Leaders also collaborate with their teams to ensure that identified goals are allocated sufficient resources—including adequate time, materials, and staff needed to implement identified strategies with fidelity to the plan. These leaders also build partnerships with external stakeholders who are able to provide additional resources and bandwidth to the school's goals.

In addition, principals are careful to work closely with district leaders to ensure that goals set at the school level are supportive of the district's priorities.

Together these levers create the foundation that allows schools to implement consistent and high-quality learning experiences for students and staff.

> **Once teams identify shared goals, they need to ensure that time is well planned and maximized to support the achievement of those goals.**

Operations and Systems Category Map

Lever 1: Goal Setting and Implementation

Schools track clear and focused goals and adjust strategies based on progress

Actions

- **Goals and Priorities:** Create clear goals and identify priority areas
- **Action Plans:** Create action plans and strategies to attain goals, and establish milestones to monitor progress to goals

Lever 2: Time Management

School leaders align the use of time to make progress toward and attain schoolwide goals

Actions

- **Time and Schedule Review:** Assess how time is allocated and used
- **Master Schedule:** Use schedule to maximize instructional time and access to rigorous content

Lever 3:
Budget

Schools align budget, external partnerships, and facilities to the strategic plan

Actions

- **Budget and Resources:** Create a budget and plan to manage resources
- **External Partnerships:** Create external partnerships that support the schoolwide goals and priority areas
- **Facilities:** Manage the facilities to ensure that students are safe and that the school is set up to facilitate learning

Lever 4: Community
and District Relations

School leaders manage the district context and school system relations to ensure a focus on learning

Actions

- **Stakeholder Communications:** Build and manage systems for stakeholder, family, and community engagement
- **District Relationships:** Build and manage district relationships

LEVER 1: Goal setting and implementation

	PRINCIPAL ACTIONS
STAGE 1	Assess the current state of the school and identify gaps that need to be addressed by analyzing student achievement data, teacher effectiveness data, and school practices
	Determine the few and focused priorities for the current year using the results of the data analysis; limit any new initiatives to those that will receive adequate resources and time for implementation and monitoring
	Regularly review data and completion of action plan items to assess progress toward goals and to adjust strategies as needed
STAGE 2	Develop a three-year strategic plan that delineates clear yearly targets and milestones that align to the districtwide goals
	Identify leadership team members who are responsible and accountable for the implementation of aspects of the strategic plan
	Set milestones and benchmarks for implementation and student progress (e.g., interim assessments, attendance) in the school improvement plan
STAGE 3	Cocreate annual goals and a school improvement plan with a broad group of stakeholders before the school year starts
	Use annual data, interim and formative data, and school improvement plan milestones to monitor, track, and review progress—systematically adjusting strategies where needed

OPERATIONS AND PLANNING LEVER 1

ACTION 1: Goals and Priorities

SCHOOL ACTIONS
Staff and families share their perspectives on school needs and performance to inform school goals A strategic plan and priorities are in place and aligned to the urgent goal of making dramatic gains in student achievement
Strategic plan priorities are public and easily accessed by multiple stakeholders Each priority area has assigned staff responsible for implementation who share common understanding of short- and long-term goals, strategies, and timelines
The leadership team uses trend data to determine grade-level targets Targets for student subgroups and grade-level cohorts are included in the school improvement plan, with milestones and benchmarks to track progress toward goals Each teacher's targets are clearly aligned to the school's goals

LEVER 1

OPERATIONS AND PLANNING

LEVER 1: Goal setting and implementation

PRINCIPAL ACTIONS
STAGE 1 Identify clear actions and strategies to make progress toward priority areas identified in the strategic plan At least two times per year, review student data and progress against strategically planned school practices and financial and operational information
STAGE 2 Link each strategy to metrics with which to measure progress against each strategic priority area Revise plans and priorities based on data in order to reach student outcome goals
STAGE 3 Lead an ongoing planning process and multiple reviews of progress against plans each year, engaging all staff (e.g., summer retreat) Lead formal reviews of progress against the strategic plan and milestones at least two times a year, in addition to conducting regular reviews of school data

OPERATIONS AND PLANNING · LEVER 1

ACTION 2: **Action Plans**

SCHOOL ACTIONS
Milestones and benchmarks are commonly known
Grade-level and content-area teams use the action plans to inform their planning
Milestones and benchmarks are commonly known and clearly tracked; if they are not met, contingency plans are created to reach the required result
Progress is regularly tracked using leading indicators
The leadership team uses available evidence and data to adjust strategies and action plans
The leadership team has institutionalized the practice of reviewing key data at every meeting
The leadership team meets regularly (at least once per week) to analyze a consistent set of key school indicators, including individual student-, classroom-, and grade-level data
The leadership team creates short- and medium-term action plans to address areas of concern and recognize areas of success

LEVER 2: Time management

	PRINCIPAL ACTIONS
STAGE 1	Review the existing schedule to assess how time is used and any areas where additional time may be available
	Assess the speed and efficiency of transition times to identify instructional time that can be recaptured through improvement of processes
	Gather data on frequency of interruptions to class time
	Review your personal schedule to assess priority of time use for classroom observation, teacher team meetings, and family communication
STAGE 2	Ensure that time blocks, rotating days, and house or community structures are serving student needs and do not focus on the needs of adults
	Work with members of the leadership team to implement a classroom observation schedule that supports new and struggling teachers
	Delegate tasks and "first-response" responsibilities to others to maintain a focus on instructional leadership
STAGE 3	Use student learning data and teacher input to identify needs that are not being met with the current schedule

ACTION 1: Time and Schedule Review

SCHOOL ACTIONS
Staff members are asked to reflect on the effectiveness of the calendar and weekly schedule
Insights and recommendations from the schedule and calendar review processes are publicly shared
Leadership team members lead components of the schedule assessment based on their areas of responsibility
Leadership team members conduct frequent classroom observations for new and struggling teachers
School staff know and access first points of contact besides the principal for a range of key needs and requests
Staff members find and improve inefficiencies in their classrooms and make suggestions that support schoolwide improvements

LEVER 2: Time management

	PRINCIPAL ACTIONS
STAGE 1	Create a daily/weekly schedule aligned to strategic priorities and focused on student needs: • Establish multiple times per week for collaborative teacher planning time • Develop clear class intervention schedules and credit recovery schedules • Ensure that the schedule meets district and state requirements for ELL and special education instruction Create extra time in the school day for core subjects; students not yet achieving at grade level receive additional instruction time (e.g., create two literacy periods—one to teach at grade level and one to teach developing skills for those not on grade level) Establish a calendar of all professional development, assessments, and key decision points for student interventions based on assessment results Create a personal calendar that builds in time for teacher observations
STAGE 2	Create with members of the leadership team a master schedule and calendar that includes key dates for data-driven instruction, student intervention, major professional opportunities, and talent reviews Create opportunities for all students to have access to arts and physical education Create a personal calendar that builds in time for teacher observations and that protects your ability to be present during arrival and dismissal times (High school) Develop a schedule that allows all students access to college preparatory and advanced courses
STAGE 3	Use student learning data and teacher input to adjust the schedule as needed to maximize time spent on learning and to ensure that all students are given ample time to make up any missed coursework On the basis of frequent reviews of student-level data, continually adjust the school calendar and schedule to match shifting priorities and needs

ACTION 2: Master Schedule

School has a detailed and consistent schedule of teacher team meetings, leadership team meetings, class schedules, and intervention activities, including staff and students involved in each

Class time for learning and teaching is maximized, with few to no interruptions

Staff have a calendar of major assessments and professional development activities that include cycles of lesson observations, coaching, and mentoring

Calendar is not paper based, and updates and edits are instantly shared on a platform or system accessible to families

Leadership team members manage and make public a detailed daily/weekly schedule of classes, curriculum focus (such as literacy blocks), student interventions, teacher team meetings, and professional development sessions

The master schedule accounts for student course requests, takes graduation requirements and credit accumulation into account, and creates a daily/weekly schedule for staff professional learning aligned to strategic priorities

Staff help develop the detailed calendar for the semester and a tentative calendar for the school year prior to its start

The master schedule comprises individualized student schedules that include accommodations for myriad different student needs, including extra time in a subject and smaller class size

The schedule supports student development in areas beyond the school day

LEVER 2

OPERATIONS AND PLANNING

LEVER 3: Budget

	PRINCIPAL ACTIONS
STAGE 1	Conduct a comprehensive review of *all* current resources (financial, staff, in-kind, supplemental, external partners/programs/resources)—and, wherever possible, shift existing resources to align to strategic priorities Identify key partners in the school and the system to support the budgeting process
STAGE 2	Forecast new resources and materials needed two to three years out based on the strategic plan (e.g., robust classroom libraries to increase literacy skills of students) and begin purchasing and planning for these needs
STAGE 3	Effectively leverage all potential resource sources through an ongoing, active approach to budget and resource management

ACTION 1: Budget and Resources

SCHOOL ACTIONS
School resources are reallocated to support strategic priorities
Staff support the alignment of resources to support strategic priorities
New resources and external partnerships are adequate to fund professional development and student intervention time and skills

OPERATIONS AND PLANNING   LEVER 3

LEVER 3: Budget

	PRINCIPAL ACTIONS
STAGE 1	Review existing community partnerships to assess their current impact on the school
	Introduce partners to the school's priority areas to ensure alignment between partner and school
	If partners are unable to adapt to a focus on high-priority areas, reframe, eliminate, or replace the partnership
STAGE 2	With the leadership team, actively seek and cultivate external partners to fill gaps or enhance and extend programming—all in support of schoolwide goals
STAGE 3	Collaborate with external partners to create explicit links to the schoolwide goals

ACTION 2: External Partnerships

SCHOOL ACTIONS
Criteria are established to review and identify partnerships, including alignment to the strategic priorities and identified student support needs of the school
External partners and programs are aligned with the school's key goals around student achievement and social-emotional development Partners are clear that their work aligns to the school's goals
External partners and programs have demonstrated impact on the school's progress toward achieving key goals External partners are fully invested in the school's success

OPERATIONS AND PLANNING   LEVER 3

LEVER 3: Budget

PRINCIPAL ACTIONS
STAGE 1 Conduct a facilities survey prior to the start of school; assess and prioritize immediately needed repairs and desired improvements Create systems to maintain the building's safety and cleanliness Develop a crisis management plan which ensures that all students and staff are safe in the event of an emergency
STAGE 2 Identify a few ways to creatively use and manipulate space to support academic priorities and initiatives
STAGE 3 Continually assess the ways in which space is used to maximize learning

OPERATIONS AND PLANNING   LEVER 3

THE SCHOOL LEADERSHIP PLAYBOOK: A FIELD GUIDE FOR DRAMATIC IMPROVEMENT

ACTION 3: Facilities

SCHOOL ACTIONS
School buildings are clean and safe; all basic facilities (bathrooms, windows, sinks, locks) are in working order; there are no "broken windows" or safety hazards
The school participates in regular safety drills
The school participates in regular crisis management drills, and all staff are familiar with procedures
The physical plant supports major academic priorities and initiatives (e.g., reading nooks, improved library, enhanced computer lab, comfortable staff lounge/meeting area)
The entire physical plant (common spaces, classrooms, hallways, resource rooms) visually and materially supports and advances schoolwide goals and initiatives

LEVER 3

OPERATIONS AND PLANNING

LEVER 4: Community and district relations

	PRINCIPAL ACTIONS
STAGE 1	Map community leaders and key political relationships
	Share the school vision and strategic plan with community and political leaders to engage their support
STAGE 2	Develop an initial plan to communicate with key community leaders and families; the plan should include a communication calendar, key messages, audiences, communication media, timeline for rollout, and staff responsibilities for executing the plan
	Incorporate community and family input into the school's plan for improvement and growth
	Build staff capacity to build meaningful relationships with community members and all stakeholders
STAGE 3	Actively involve community leaders and families in planning for the school
	Put structures and processes in place to consistently partner with stakeholders, including staff, families, and students, to inform and adjust strategies

ACTION 1: Stakeholder Communications

SCHOOL ACTIONS
Community leaders and families receive consistent communication about key school events and information
Structures are in place to ensure that all stakeholders have multiple opportunities to engage in a dialogue with members of school leadership
Communications from stakeholders are responded to in a timely manner, with appropriate tone and a tailored message
The leadership team drives key messages to internal and external stakeholders
Stakeholders have multiple ways to communicate with all staff in addition to key leadership
Community participation is evident in multiple aspects of the school
Stakeholders and community members have multiple ways and opportunities to become involved in the school

LEVER 4

OPERATIONS AND PLANNING

LEVER 4: Community and district relations

	PRINCIPAL ACTIONS
STAGE 1	Proactively share the school vision and strategic plan with the district/school system manager Share priority areas for the year as well as the rationale for each priority area
STAGE 2	Establish a clear message to the district/system manager around strategic plans; create confidence and "buffer" from system management to allow staff to implement specific strategies and elements outlined in the plan Maintain constant contact with the district office to share successes and challenges
STAGE 3	Anticipate opportunities where district management can advocate on behalf of the school

OPERATIONS AND PLANNING   LEVER 4

ACTION 2: District Relationships

SCHOOL ACTIONS
School system managers receive consistent communication about key school events and information
Principal supervisors have a clear understanding of the school's areas for growth
The strategic plan uses established district process for school planning
District strategies and initiatives that directly support the school are built into the strategic plan
The district/system manager has a clear sense of the school's plans and is a strong advocate for the school

Personal Leadership

PERSONAL LEADERSHIP DESCRIBES SPECIFIC ACTIONS PRINCIPALS CAN take to inspire, support, and galvanize the school communities they lead in the face of ongoing challenges. Through our leader development programs and our research analyzing leader practices, we have determined that a principal's skills at working with and leading others are key factors in driving student achievement gains, successfully managing adults, and navigating the politics of a school system.

Effective leaders intentionally use their belief in the students and the school to hold themselves and others to high expectations. They take every opportunity possible to bring hope to their school community, model high expectations for students, and develop teacher effectiveness. We describe this collective set of leadership skills as personal leadership—key actions that speak to the principal's overall belief, intent, and approach to students, staff, families, and community members.

The Personal Leadership category is divided into five levers that describe the personal leadership behaviors that support school success:

- Belief-based, goal-driven leadership

- Equity-focused leadership

- Interpersonal leadership

- Adaptive leadership

- Resilient leadership

In essence, the principal's leadership style must strike a balance between being very firm about nonnegotiable goals—clear expectations established, supported, and monitored so that all students and staff can do their work better—and demonstrating genuine engagement with others, humility, and relationship building.

Some argue that components of these actions are dispositions that are innate in a subset of leaders, but we believe that over time and with ongoing feedback and reflection, leaders can develop and build the skills needed to consistently demonstrate the actions described in this category.

> A principal's skills at working with and leading others are key factors in driving student achievement gains, successfully managing adults, and navigating the politics of a district system.

TRANSFORMATIONAL PRINCIPALS IN ACTION

Claudia Aguirre

When Claudia Aguirre became the principal at Dual Language Middle School in New York City, it had been known as a "dumping ground" for low-performing students; more than 90 percent of students were living in poverty, more than 30 percent of students were English language learners, and more than 25 percent were designated "special education." It was not uncommon for some students to arrive at the school not fluent in either English or Spanish. Aguirre knew she had a limited amount of time to prepare her students for high school, and took on the challenge of building belief among the students and the staff that they could succeed. She built strong relationships with the families and the students and saw improvements in attendance as they began to see her as an advocate and ally who would support successful high school entry.

To build a sense of possibility, she outlined goals and expectations for every teacher and student. She made sure that every staff member and student knew the number of days they had left at Dual Language before high school. She used the countdown to demonstrate her relentless belief that all students can achieve at high levels and to keep the urgency to change and develop effective instructional practice when teachers bristled at the high expectations. She offered supports and specific strategies while not compromising when teachers did not improve. She was transparent that teachers needed to demonstrate progress and developed individualized curriculum to support their growth.

 ## STRUCTURE

The other categories of the TLF describe principal actions that align to a school's current state. The Personal Leadership category outlines key actions the leader must implement through *all* stages of school development.

The actions described in the Personal Leadership category have been observed across multiple schools as levers that allow leaders to maintain focus on the school's vision to improve student performance. This is the only category for which we do not include school stages, to emphasize that leaders need to implement these actions no matter how the school is currently performing.

The manner in which these principal actions are implemented may change as the school improves and as more systems and structures are in place, but throughout their time as principal, leaders must model personal leadership in their actions.

 ## LEVERS IN THE PERSONAL LEADERSHIP CATEGORY

As noted earlier, the levers within the Personal Leadership category describe the consistent actions that effective principals take to inspire their school communities toward a common set of beliefs and goals, support their communities through the changes necessary to reach higher levels of student achievement, and build their capacity to remove barriers and overcome setbacks on the path of improvement. These levers and the detailed actions within them support all of the other actions throughout the framework.

Belief-Based and Goal-Driven Leadership

Strong leaders demonstrate an unwavering belief in the ability of all children to achieve at high levels—they inspire the staff with a sense of possibility and a concrete pathway to realize the school's vision. They set ambitious but achievable goals and keep all members of the school community focused on achieving them. Further, they hold themselves personally responsible for attaining the school goals.

Equity-Focused Leadership

We recognize that leaders must consciously strive to create an inclusive environment that removes limits that have prevented all groups of students from being successful in school. Such an effort begins with every leader developing an understanding of his or her individual biases and perceptions as well as the ways in which he or she is perceived by others. It includes actively addressing statements of bias, cultural incompetence, or prejudice to ensure that the school is a safe and supportive place for all students.

Interpersonal Leadership

To create change in a school, a leader builds strong and trusting relationships with multiple stakeholder groups. The leader develops and models strong communication skills that are always

Personal Leadership Category Map

**Lever 1: Belief-Based
and Goal-Driven
Leadership**

*Leader consistently
demonstrates belief
that every student can
achieve at high levels*

**Lever 2:
Equity-Focused
Leadership**

*Leader continuously
dismantles inequitable
and exclusionary
practices and creates
a fully inclusive
environment where
all children
and adults thrive and
learn at high levels*

**Lever 3:
Interpersonal
Leadership**

*Leader builds
trusting relationships
and facilitates
engaged communities
of adults and
students dedicated
to reaching
school goals*

**Lever 4:
Adaptive
Leadership**

*Leader mobilizes
others to resolve
challenges
requiring changes
in values, beliefs,
assumptions, and
habits of behavior*

**Lever 5:
Resilient
Leadership**

*Leader demonstrates
self-awareness,
ongoing learning,
and resiliency in the
service of continuous
improvement*

respectful. Leaders tailor their messages to address the questions and the needs of each key stakeholder group and individual.

Adaptive Leadership

Leaders help their teams, families, and students navigate changes to the school landscape while maintaining a focus on the vision that the community has agreed on. They facilitate experiences that inspire changes in values, beliefs, assumptions, and habits of behavior that do not support school and student success. Whether changes are initiated by the leader, the community, or the district, the leader recognizes the emotions that accompany change and leads processes that support the school community through initial discomfort as they make shifts in practice that will improve student outcomes.

Resilient Leadership

Resilient leaders demonstrate resolve in the face of adversity and challenge. They constantly look for solutions that will move the school closer to its goals. Leaders also reflect on their actions; they consciously use feedback and criticism to improve their leadership.

LEVER 1: Belief-based and goal-driven leadership

Leader consistently demonstrates belief that every student can achieve at high levels

Set high but achievable goals for students

Focus decisions on student needs, not adult outcomes

Create and maintain schoolwide urgency to improve school outcomes

Demonstrate personal commitment to ensuring high academic achievement for all students

Inspire a schoolwide sense of positivism and possibility

Hold self and others accountable for outcomes

LEVER 2: Equity-focused leadership

Leader continuously dismantles inequitable and exclusionary practices and creates a fully inclusive environment where all children and adults thrive and learn at high levels

Break down barriers to student learning that stem from structural and institutional biases

Foster equity and inclusion by consistently addressing the dynamics of power within the community

Seek out and engage diverse perspectives to build an effective organization

Demonstrate a commitment to reflect on how your personal biases and privileges impact your actions, and create learning opportunities and a supportive culture for others to do the same

Initiate direct conversations about equity and bias to build the school's collective capacity

Lead professional development and create learning opportunities from moments of cultural incompetence or conflict

LEVER 3: Interpersonal leadership

Leader builds trusting relationships and facilitates engaged communities of adults and students dedicated to reaching school goals

Be transparent about expectations with all stakeholders and treat all stakeholders with respect—even those who may not share the same beliefs

Create a culture that facilitates the development of trusting relationships

Motivate and inspire individuals and communicate their value to the school

Seek multiple perspectives from key stakeholders, to predict and plan strategic actions

Select appropriate facilitation and leadership strategies when leading groups of people; these should balance appropriate communication strategies for diverse constituents and contexts (e.g., active listening, seeking feedback)

LEVER 4: Adaptive leadership

Leader mobilizes others to resolve challenges requiring changes in values, beliefs, assumptions, and habits of behavior

Identify root causes and adaptive challenges that need to be resolved

Take risks to challenge existing school and district/charter management organization practices, policies, and traditions—including those that you have created—that do not have a positive impact on student achievement

Identify and build on the existing school and community strengths that have positive impact on student achievement

Establish and maintain a sustainable level of urgency and ongoing learning needed to tackle adaptive challenges

Recognize and manage the emotions of change, including resistance, fear, and loss

Address the stages of the change process and support staff as they face challenges and implementation dips

Sequencing note: In order to do the difficult work of adaptive change management, building organizational and relational trust, as described in Lever 3, is an essential foundation.

PERSONAL LEADERSHIP   LEVER 4

LEVER 5: Resilient leadership

Leader demonstrates self-awareness, ongoing learning, and resiliency in the service of continuous improvement

Demonstrate personal resolve and maintain core confidence and belief in self and the school even in the face of adversity

Continuously reflect on performance, seek feedback, and actively pursue opportunities to improve personal leadership and the school

Take initiative and remain solutions oriented at all times to move the work of the school forward

Proactively build professional and personal supports—including adequate personal time—necessary for sustaining school leadership over time

CONCLUSION

PRINCIPALS ARE ASKED TO DIAGNOSE CHALLENGES and prescribe treatments in constantly evolving environments. Derived from effective practices and lessons learned from school leaders across the country, the TLF serves as an outline that can help principals navigate the changing landscape of their school more successfully. The categories and actions of the TLF provide leaders with critical guideposts on the pathway to improved student outcomes.

Although the framework presents key areas separately to distill and highlight specific ideas, we know that schools only function when the categories work in concert. To successfully implement the school actions, leaders will have to draw on and leverage those connections. For example, teachers cannot be expected to use interim assessment data for corrective instruction if there are no systems in place to ensure that data is quickly returned to teachers. Similarly, to develop a collaborative culture, staff members need time, protocols, and clear expectations to help guide and shape their conversations.

Rather than describing all of the responsibilities placed on a leader, the framework's five categories intentionally focus on the high-leverage components necessary for school change, to help leaders remain focused on actions that will support and lead to transformational changes in student outcomes.

By using the framework, leaders can accurately assess the current state of their schools to develop precise strategies that improve student performance and teacher effectiveness. We have seen the framework implemented in a variety of contexts and by a variety of leaders; no two schools or communities have identical challenges, and this framework relies on the skill and expertise of educators who know their staff and students.

When used well, the TLF can help leaders see how their actions impact culture and instruction throughout the school. For new leaders, the framework can be a key tool for reviewing current practices, expectations, processes, and systems that will allow these leaders to plan for and implement successful entry. It can also help leaders identify staff aligned to their vision, so that capacity building and succession planning can begin even in year 1. For leaders who have demonstrated improvements during their tenure, the framework can be used to review and revise tactics to move to higher stages of school action in each category, resulting in continued improvements in student outcomes. More experienced leaders can use the TLF to help identify and address root causes behind long-lasting trends within the school. Or they may use it to reflect on moments when their leadership has helped or hindered the school. Regardless of a leader's tenure, the framework supports effective leadership and school improvement.

By following the principles outlined in the TLF, leaders across the country have propelled their schools to greater student achievement gains, enriching the experience of students and educators alike. We hope that after reading this book, you, too, feel ready to use the framework to improve student performance in your own school or district. Please share with us your experiences by emailing us at playbookstories@newleaders.org.

Methodology of the New Leaders Research Study

THE FINDINGS OUTLINED IN THIS BOOK DRAW from an extensive review of the available research on the practices of effective schools, turnaround schools, secondary schools, and leadership. In that initial review, we found descriptions of excellence in high-poverty schools, but less data on how leaders transformed those schools into centers of excellence.

To determine what leadership and school practices distinguished schools that were obtaining dramatic gains in student achievement from schools that were obtaining incremental gains, we looked into the New Leaders community for schools that experienced dramatic gains and matched them with schools that had similar profiles but only incremental gains. Dramatic gains were defined as combined gains in percent proficient in math and English language arts of 20 points or more. Incremental gains were defined as combined gains in percent proficient in math and English language arts of 3 to 10 points.

We brought those initial findings to a group of experts comprising New Leaders staff, principals, and leaders in the education reform field, who reviewed that data and identified the high-level categories of the framework. In subsequent years, we continued to conduct leader interviews, case studies, and site visits. Over the course of the study, the data set grew to include over one hundred case studies, interviews, and site visits from schools across the country.

In addition, New Leaders completed a review of all resources available through New Leaders' Effective Practice Incentive Community (EPIC). EPIC was a New Leaders initiative that identified schools that made the most impressive gains, and rewarded those school leaders and teachers for sharing the practices that led to the gains. The EPIC data set consists of case studies of New Leaders and non–New Leaders schools that had relatively higher value-added scores than other schools in their district or charter consortium.

Both studies explored the following questions:

1. What specific actions do principals of high-gaining schools take to improve student achievement?
2. What specific actions do principals of high-gaining schools take to improve teacher effectiveness?
3. What distinguishes principals of high-gaining schools from other principals?
4. What school practices are evident in high-gaining schools?

GLOSSARY

ACTION PLANS

Action plans are created to address priority areas identified by leaders and schools. They are detailed documents that are intended to meet short- and longer-term priorities and goals. Action planning clarifies strategic goals and priorities for all members of the school staff and community so that human and fiscal resources are used effectively schoolwide. Action plans should include a set of specific activities; persons responsible for implementing each activity; resources needed to conduct each activity; a timeline for completing each activity; and benchmarks for measuring success or lack of success of each activity.

BEHAVIORAL EXPECTATIONS

Behavioral expectations outline required conduct for students and staff. A strong set of expectations explicitly describes how positive behaviors are rewarded and the consequences for poor behavior that is not aligned to the school's values. Rewards and consequences are clearly in alignment with the vision, mission, and values identified by the school.

BEHAVIORS

Behaviors are specific age-appropriate actions that are derived from the school's specific vision, mission, and values. These behaviors describe what success looks like in the context and setting of the school and along the continuum of student development. These behaviors are described and taught and are clear to both adults and students.

BUDGET RESOURCES

Although resources often focus on finances, the framework includes time, materials, and staff allocations as well to describe the multiple tools the leader can use to support the school goals and to improve student achievement.

CULTURAL COMPETENCE

Cultural competence requires that organizations

- Have a defined set of values and principles, and demonstrate behaviors, attitudes, policies, and structures that enable them to work effectively cross-culturally.

- Have the capacity to (1) value diversity, (2) conduct self-assessment, (3) manage the dynamics of difference, (4) acquire and institutionalize cultural knowledge, and (5) adapt to diversity and the cultural contexts of communities they serve.

- Incorporate the above in all aspects of policymaking, administration, practice, and service delivery, and systematically involve consumers, families, and communities.

Cultural competence is a developmental process that evolves over an extended period. Both individuals and organizations are at various levels of awareness, knowledge, and skills along the cultural competence continuum (National Center for Cultural Competence, http://nccc.georgetown.edu/foundations/frameworks.html, adapted from Cross, Bazron, Dennis, & Isaacs, 1989).

CURRICULUM MAP

The curriculum map is a chart or plan that outlines the arc of content that students need to learn over the course of the year. The plan outlines how one unit deepens and builds on the content from earlier units. It also includes a vertical articulation of how the learning from one year will develop from one year to the next.

DATA-DRIVEN INSTRUCTION

Data-driven instruction is the practice of using multiple forms of data to guide pacing and instructional strategies. It places the focus on student learning and allows teachers to modify their teaching to meet student needs. Using data to shape instruction holds teachers accountable for what was learned as opposed to what was taught.

DIFFERENTIATION

Differentiated instruction is well organized and well planned, and addresses not only different ability levels but also the different needs, interests, and strengths of learners. Differentiation of instruction allows for whole-group instruction, heterogeneous small-group cooperative work, and individual instruction. It allows the teacher to create student-centered learning experiences that focus on varied approaches to content, process, and product. In addition, it provides for ongoing, embedded, authentic assessment of students' skills, interests, and learning style (Tomlinson, 2005).

EFFICACY

Efficacy as a formal academic term focuses on how the future-oriented belief about the level of competence a person expects that he or she will display in a given situation impacts his or her performance (Bandura, 1997). In other words, staff or students who believe they will be competent at a task—or can become competent through ongoing learning and feedback—will perform at higher levels. This belief in the ability to become competent also connects to the research of Carol Dweck (2000) and her description of the "growth mindset." Individuals with this growth mindset see competence as something that can be developed and not as an innate quality, and therefore they are not discouraged when they have setbacks and make mistakes. Instead, they use those setbacks as feedback to improve, and believe that ongoing practice and hard work are the keys to success.

We have seen repeatedly in our work with schools that building this sense of efficacy for staff and students—and an orientation to the growth mindset—is a crucial element of effective school cultures.

INTERVENTIONS

Supports and services implemented for students who have been assessed to be currently below grade level and/or are at risk of not meeting the standards for their grade. Supports may include classroom-based intervention services or supplemental supports that occur outside of class time to meet the instructional needs of individual students as determined by the results of diagnostic assessments.

INSTRUCTIONAL LEADERSHIP TEAM

The instructional leadership team leads the core instructional work of the school and is tasked to improve the quality of instruction. The team analyzes formative and summative student learning data, identifies trends, and discusses strategies for reteaching or intervention. They make key decisions about the school's curriculum and provide support to teachers. Members of the instructional leadership team serve as the leaders of regular teacher team meetings, where they help all teachers conduct similar analyses of data and student work and identify strategies for improvement. In the Talent Management category, we discuss leadership team members evaluating teachers; this is not possible in all contexts. When members of the team do evaluate teachers, they are most often certified administrators. The team usually comprises full-time school staff, including teacher leaders, instructional coaches, and assistant principals.

In some schools, this team may be distinct from a school leadership team that includes additional stakeholders, such as family members or community leaders. (See definition of *leadership team* below.)

LEADERSHIP TEAM

Leadership team members are responsible for implementing schoolwide initiatives, modeling cultural norms, and supporting the school's vision. The leadership team plays a key role in working with the principal to identify priorities, goals, and action plans to support school improvement.

In some schools, the leadership team is not distinct from the instructional leadership team (see glossary entry), but leadership teams may comprise additional stakeholders, including parents, community members, and other staff. In some districts, the makeup of the leadership team is mandated by the district and/or is negotiated as part of the collective bargaining agreement. In those cases, the leader may be limited in terms of who serves as a member of the team.

MASTERY EXPERIENCES

Mastery experiences, as we define them, are rigorous academic projects that ask students to demonstrate mastery of a particular skill or content area. Beyond just serving as assessments of student knowledge and skill, these mastery experiences play an important role in building student efficacy and school culture. Teachers spend significant time planning for these projects and setting rigorous expectations for students' demonstration, and they also provide robust supports to help all students succeed in demonstrating mastery in at least one major project. The ongoing feedback throughout the process of doing the project—and the eventual success for students at the end—are powerful elements in developing a student's sense of efficacy and the belief that hard work and repeated attempts will lead to eventual success.

NONNEGOTIABLES

In determining schoolwide goals and priorities, leaders often identify three to five nonnegotiables—ideas, principles, or strategies that will be adhered to throughout the year. In naming these areas of focus, the leader creates clear expectations of what staff and students need to work toward, and they help the team maintain focused on a narrow set of goals.

ON TRACK/OFF TRACK

These terms refer to research-based indicators that have been shown to predict eventual graduation of secondary students. As defined in research from the Consortium on Chicago School Research, a freshman student is defined as "on track" if he or she has at least five credits by the end of the year and no more than one semester F in a core class. Additional research by the Consortium and others has also shown the importance of tracking attendance as a key predictor of on-track status, along with course grades. The Consortium's research in Chicago has shown that schools that regularly track data about which students are on track and off track and then take action during the freshman and sophomore years to address the individual student challenges demonstrate significant increases in four-year graduation rates (Allensworth, 2007).

PREVENTIONS

Providing proactive targeted instruction or services for students who are struggling with particular content within a subject that if left unaddressed could lead to additional challenges and/or result in lower performance.

PROFESSIONAL LEARNING COMMUNITY

Professional learning communities comprise educators who work collaboratively to improve academic experiences for students and educators through an ongoing process of job-embedded collective inquiry and action research.

RETEACHING

Reteaching, which New Leaders now describes as corrective instruction, is a critical part of the data-driven instructional cycle: adults identify what students have not yet learned, build these concepts into their scope and sequence, and teach the concepts differently.

SCAFFOLD

Developed as a metaphor to describe the type of assistance offered by a teacher or peer to support learning, scaffolding helps the student master a task or concept that the student is initially unable to grasp independently. The teacher offers assistance with only those skills that are beyond the student's capability. Of great importance is allowing the student to complete unassisted as much of the task as possible. "Scaffolding is actually a bridge used to build upon what students already know to arrive at something they do not know. If scaffolding is properly administered, it will act as an enabler, not as a disabler" (Benson, 1997).

SCOPE AND SEQUENCE

This term describes a framework that brings together instructional standards, key ideas, and performance indicators organized by grade. Each grade is organized around suggested time frames for the teaching of core content (units of study) guided by essential questions.

SOCIAL-EMOTIONAL SKILLS

These skills help students recognize and manage emotions, care about others, make good decisions, behave ethically and responsibly, develop positive relationships, and avoid negative behaviors. When students develop social-emotional skills, they enhance their ability to integrate thinking, feeling, and behaving in order to achieve important life tasks. Students demonstrate several characteristics as they develop their social-emotional skills, including self-esteem, sense of purpose, resiliency, control over their future, and aptitude for building relationships.

SUPPORTIVE ADULT-STUDENT RELATIONSHIPS

Adults take responsibility to create and build strong, positive, and respectful relationships with students to ensure that all students receive support for their academic progress and their broader social-emotional development.

TWENTY-FIRST-CENTURY SKILLS

These are the skills students need to survive in the digital age and succeed in the modern economy; competencies include collaboration, digital literacy, critical thinking, and problem solving. They go beyond the academic skills that have traditionally been targeted and assessed by state and district-level assessments, though some of these skills are starting to be addressed by new academic standards and assessments in multiple states. Among a number of writers and organizations that have offered definitions of twenty-first-century skills, two frequently cited summaries are "21st Century Student Outcomes" (Partnership for 21st Century Skills, 2011) and the "Four Keys to College and Career Readiness" (Conley, 2012).

VALUES

Values are a set of principles derived from the vision and mission; they guide the definitions of specific behaviors and a code of conduct. For example, the value "be respectful" might come from the vision and mission for the school and then be translated into specific behaviors described in the behavioral expectations—that is, ways to demonstrate respectful behavior.

BIBLIOGRAPHY AND WORKS CITED

Aladjem, D. K., Birman, B. F., Orland, M., Harr-Robins, J., Heredia, A., Parrish, T. B., & Ruffini, S. J. (2010). *Achieving dramatic school improvement: An exploratory study*. Washington, DC: US Department of Education.

Allensworth, E., & Easton, J. (2007, July). *What matters for staying on-track and graduating from Chicago public high schools*. Chicago, IL: University of Chicago, Consortium on Chicago School Research.

Allensworth, E., Ponisciak, S., & Mazzeo, C. (2009). The schools teachers leave: Teacher mobility in Chicago public schools. Chicago, IL: Consortium on Chicago School Research.

Augustine, C. H., Gonzalez, G., Ikemoto, G. S., Russell, J., Zellman, G. L., Constant, L., … Dembosky, J. W. (2009). *Improving school leadership: The promise of cohesive leadership systems*. Santa Monica, CA: RAND.

Baker, B. D., & Cooper, B. C. (2005). Do principals with stronger academic backgrounds hire better teachers? Policy implications for improving high-poverty schools. *Educational Administration Quarterly*, 41, 449–479.

Balu, R., Horng, E. L., & Loeb, S. (2010). *Strategic personnel management: How school principals recruit, retain, develop and remove teachers* (School Leadership Research, Working Paper 10-6). Stanford, CA: Institute for Research on Education Policy and Practice.

Bambrick-Santoyo, P. (2012). *Leverage leadership: A practical guide to building exceptional schools*. San Francisco, CA: Jossey-Bass.

Bandura, A. (1994). Self-efficacy. In V. S. Ramachaudran (Ed.), *Encyclopedia of human behavior* (Vol. 4, pp. 71–81). New York, NY: Academic Press.

Barber, M., Whelan, F., & Clark, M. (2010). *Capturing the leadership premium: How the world's top school systems are building leadership capacity for the future*. New York, NY: McKinsey & Company.

Becker, B. E., Huselid, M. E., & Ulrich, D. (2001). *The HR scorecard: Linking people, strategy, and performance*. Boston, MA: Harvard Business School Press.

Benson, B. (1997). Scaffolding (Coming to terms). *English Journal*, 86(7), 126–127.

Beteille, T., Kalogrides, D., & Loeb, S. (2009). *Effective schools: Managing the recruitment, development, and retention of high-quality teachers*. Washington, DC: National Center for Analysis of Longitudinal Data in Education Research.

Black, P., & Wiliam, D. (1998). Assessment and classroom learning. *Assessment in Education*, 5, 7–74.

Blase, J., & Blase, J. (1999). Principals' instructional leadership and teacher development: Teachers' perspectives. *Educational Administration Quarterly*, 35, 349–378.

Boyd, D. J., Grossman, P. L., Ing, M., Lankford, H., Loeb, S., & Wyckoff, J. H. (2009). *The influence of school administrators on teacher retention decisions* (CALDER Working Papers). Washington, DC: National Center for Analysis of Longitudinal Data in Education Research.

Branch, G., Hanushek, E. A., & Rivkin, S. G. (2009). *Estimating principal effectiveness* (CALDER Working Papers). Washington, DC:

National Center for Analysis of Longitudinal Data in Education Research.

Branch, G., Hanushek, E. A., & Rivkin, S. G. (2012). *Estimating the effect of leaders on public sector productivity: The case of school principals.* Washington, DC: National Center for Analysis of Longitudinal Data in Education Research.

Bredeson, P. V. (2013). Distributed instructional leadership in urban high schools: Transforming the work of principals and department chairs through professional development. *Journal of School Leadership, 23*, 362–385.

Bryk, A. S., Sebring, P. B., Allensworth, E., Luppescu, S., & Easton, J. Q. (2010). *Organizing schools for improvement: Lessons from Chicago.* Chicago, IL: University of Chicago Press.

Burkhauser, S., Gates, S. M., Hamilton, L., & Ikemoto, G. S. (2012). *First-year principals in urban school districts: How actions and working conditions relate to outcomes.* Santa Monica, CA: RAND.

Campbell, C., & Gross, B. (2008). *Working without a safety net: How charter school leaders can best survive on the high wire.* Seattle, WA: National Charter School Research Project, Center on Reinventing Public Education.

Chenoweth, K., & Theokas, C. (2011). *Getting it done: Leading academic success in unexpected schools.* Cambridge, MA: Harvard Education Press.

Clark, D., Martorell, P., & Rockoff, J. (2009). *School principals and school performance.* Washington, DC: National Center for Analysis of Longitudinal Data in Education Research.

Clotfelter, C. T., Glennie, E. J., Ladd, H. F., & Vigdor, J. L. (2008). Teacher bonuses and teacher retention in low-performing schools: Evidence from the North Carolina $1,800 teacher bonus program. *Public Finance Review, 36*, 63–87.

Clotfelter, C. T., Ladd, H. F., Vigdor, J. L., & Wheeler, J. (2007). *High-poverty schools and the distribution of teachers and principals.* Washington, DC: National Center for Analysis of Longitudinal Data in Education Research.

Collins, J. (2001). *Good to great: Why some companies make the leap . . . and others don't.* New York, NY: HarperCollins.

Conley, D. (2012, May). *A complete definition of college and career readiness.* Portland, OR: Educational Policy Improvement Center.

Copland, M. A. (2003). Leadership of inquiry: Building and sustaining capacity for school improvement. *Educational Evaluation and Policy Analysis, 25,* 375–395.

Cosner, S. (2011). Teacher learning, instructional considerations and principal communication: Lessons from a longitudinal study of collaborative data use by teachers. *Educational Management Administration & Leadership, 39,* 568–589.

Cross, T. L., Bazron, B. J., Dennis, K. W., & Isaacs, M. R. (1989, March). *Towards a culturally competent system of care: A monograph on effective services for minority children who are severely emotionally disturbed* (Vol. 1). Washington, DC: Georgetown University, Center for Child and Human Development.

Cuban, L. (1988). *The managerial imperative and the practice of leadership in schools.* Albany: State University of New York Press.

Curtis, R., & Wurtzel, J. (Eds.). (2010). *Teaching talent: A visionary framework for human capital in education.* Cambridge, MA: Harvard Education Press.

Daly, A. J., Der-Martirosian, C., Ong-Dean, C., Park, V., & Wishard-Guerra, A. (2011). Leading under sanction: Principals' perceptions of threat rigidity, efficacy, and leadership in underperforming schools. *Leadership and Policy in Schools, 10,* 171–206.

Daly, T., Keeling, D., Grainger, R., & Grundies, A. (2008). *Mutual benefits: New York City's shift to mutual consent in teacher hiring.* Brooklyn, NY: New Teacher Project.

Darling-Hammond, L., LaPointe, M., Meyerson, D., Orr, M. T., & Cohen, C. (2007). *Preparing school leaders for a changing world: Lessons from exemplary leadership development programs.* Stanford, CA: Stanford University, Stanford Educational Leadership Institute.

Donaldson, M. L. (2011). *Principals' approaches to developing teacher quality: Constraints and opportunities in hiring, assigning, evaluating, and developing teachers.* Washington, DC: Center for American Progress.

Dweck, C. (2000). *Self-theories: Their role in motivation, personality, and development* (Essays in Social Psychology). Philadelphia, PA: Psychology Press.

Economist Intelligence Unit. (2006, May). *The CEO's role in talent management: How top executives from ten countries are nurturing the leaders of tomorrow.* London, England: Author. Retrieved from http://graphics.eiu.com/files/ad_pdfs/eiu_DDI_talent _Management_WP.pdf

Fink, E., & Resnick, L. B. (2001). *Developing principals as instructional leaders.* Pittsburgh, PA: University of Pittsburgh, High Performance Learning Communities Project, Learning Research and Development Center.

Finnigan, K. S. (2012). Principal leadership in low-performing schools: A closer look through the eyes of teachers. *Education and Urban Society, 44,* 182–202.

Fullan, M. (2014). *The principal: Three keys to maximizing impact.* San Francisco, CA: Jossey-Bass.

Gates, S. M. (2010). *Advancing strategic human capital management in public education: Policy insights from the private sector and federal government experience.* Santa Monica, CA: RAND.

Georgia Leadership Institute for School Improvement. (2012). *Conditions for success: A case study of leadership practice in a rural Georgia school district.* Lawrenceville, GA: Author.

Gordon, R., Kane, T. J., & Staiger, D. O. (2006). *Identifying effective teachers using performance on the job.* Washington, DC: Brookings Institution.

Green, J., Chirichello, M., Mallory, B., Melton, T., & Lindahl, R. (2011). *Assessing leadership dispositions: Issues, challenges, and promising practices.* National Council of Professors of Education Administration. Retrieved from http://www.eric.ed.gov /PDFS/EJ974332.pdf

Grissom, J. A. (2008). But do they stay? Addressing issues of teacher retention through alternative certification. In P. Grossman & S. Loeb (Eds.), *Alternative routes to teaching: Mapping the new landscape of teacher education* (pp. 129–155). Cambridge, MA: Harvard Education Press.

Grissom, J. A., & Loeb, S. (2009). *Triangulating principal effectiveness: How perspectives of parents, teachers, and assistant principals identify the central importance of managerial skills* (CALDER Working Papers). Washington, DC: National Center for Analysis of Longitudinal Data in Education Research.

Grissom, J. A., Loeb, S., & Master, B. (2013). Effective instructional time use for school leaders: Longitudinal evidence from observations of principals. *Educational Researcher, 42,* 433–444.

Hallinger, P. (1992). The evolving role of American principals: From managerial to instructional to transformational leaders. *Journal of Educational Administration, 30*(3), 35–49.

Halverson, R. R., Grigg, J., Pritchett, R., & Thomas, C. (2007). The new instructional leadership: Creating data-driven instructional systems in schools. *Journal of School Leadership, 17,* 159–194.

Halverson, R. R., Kelley, C., & Kimball, S. (2004). Implementing teacher evaluation systems: How principals make sense of complex artifacts to shape local instructional practice. In W. K. Hoy & C. G. Miskel (Eds.), *Educational administration policy, and reform* (pp. 153–188). Greenwich, CT: Information Age.

Hansen, J., Ikemoto, G., Marsh, J., & Barney, H. (2007). *School finance systems and their responsiveness to performance pressures: A case study of North Carolina.* Santa Monica, CA: RAND.

Harris, D. N., & Sass, T. R. (2009). *What makes for a good teacher and who can tell?* (Working Paper 30). Washington, DC: Urban Institute, National Center for Analysis of Longitudinal Data in Education Research. Retrieved from http://mailer.fsu.edu/~tsass /Papers/IES%20Principal%20Eval%2017B.pdf

Heck, R. (1992). Principals' instructional leadership and school performance: Implications for policy development. *Educational Evaluation and Policy Analysis, 14,* 21–34.

Hemphill, K., & Nauer, C. (2010, June 16). *Managing by the numbers: Empowerment and accountability in New York City's schools.* New York, NY: Center for New York City Affairs and Milano the New School for Management and Urban Policy.

Hewitt, P. (2010). Retaining new teachers: Supportive principals needed. *ASCDExpress, 6*(2).

Honig, M. I. (Ed.). (2006). *New directions in education policy implementation: Confronting complexity.* Albany: State University of New York Press.

Honig, M. I. (2012). District central office leadership as teaching: How central office administrators support principals' development as instructional leaders. *Educational Administration Quarterly*, 48, 733–774. doi: 10.1177/0013161X12443258

Honig, M. I., Copland, M. A., Rainey, L., Lorton, J. A., & Newton, M. (2010). *Central office transformation for district-wide teaching and learning improvement*. Seattle: University of Washington, Center for the Study of Teaching Policy.

Honig, M. I., & Rainey, L. R. (2011). Autonomy and school improvement: What do we know and where do we go from here? *Educational Policy*. doi: 10.1177/0895904811417590

Horng, E. L., Klasik, D., & Loeb, S. (2009). *Principal time-use and school effectiveness* (CALDER Working Papers). Washington, DC: National Center for Analysis of Longitudinal Data in Education Research.

Horng, E. L., Klasik, D., & Loeb, S. (2010). Principal's time use and school effectiveness. *American Journal of Education*, 116, 491–523.

Huggins, K. S., Scheurich, J. J., & Morgan, J. R. (2011). Professional learning communities as a leadership strategy to drive math success in an urban high school serving diverse, low-income students: A case study. *Journal of Education for Students Placed at Risk*, 16, 67–88.

Huselid, M. A. (2005). *The workforce scorecard: Managing human capital to execute strategy*. Boston, MA: Harvard Business School Press.

Hutchins, D. J., Epstein, J. L., & Sheldon, S. (2012). *How do principals' reports of leadership practices reflect UEF categories, levers, and concepts?* Baltimore, MD: Johns Hopkins University, Center on School, Family, and Community Partnerships.

Ikemoto, G., Gates, S., & Hamilton, L. (2009, November). *District and school conditions associated with successful leadership in urban school districts*. Paper presented at the annual conference of the University Council of Education Administration, Anaheim, CA.

Isenberg, E., & Hock, H. (2010). *Measuring school and teacher value added for IMPACT and TEAM in DC Public Schools*. Washington, DC: Mathematica Policy Research.

Jacob, B., & Lefgren, L. (2008). Can principals identify effective teachers? Evidence on subjective performance evaluation in education. *Journal of Labor Economics, 25,* 101–136. Retrieved from http://econ.byu.edu/faculty/Lefgren/Assets/papers/principals.pdf

Jerald, C. (2012). *Leading for effective teaching: How school systems can support principal success*. Washington, DC: Bill and Melinda Gates Foundation.

Kafka, J. (2009). The principalship in historical perspective. *Peabody Journal of Education, 84,* 318–330.

Kane, T. J., & Staiger, D. O. (2008). *Estimating teacher impacts on student achievement: An experimental evaluation*. Cambridge, MA: National Bureau of Economic Research.

Katz, S., Earl, L. M., & Jaafar, S. B. (2009). *Building and connecting learning communities: The power of networks for school improvement*. Thousand Oaks, CA: Corwin.

Kimball, S. M., Milanowski, A., & Heneman, H. G., III. (2010). *Principal as human capital manager: Evidence from two large districts*. Madison, WI: Consortium for Policy Research in Education, Strategic Management of Human Capital Project.

Knapp, M. S., Copland, M. A., Honig, M. I., Plecki, M. L., & Portin, B. S. (2010). *Learning-focused leadership and leadership support: Meaning and practice in urban systems*. Seattle: University of Washington, Center for the Study of Teaching and Policy.

Ladd, H. F. (2009). *Teachers' perceptions of their working conditions: How predictive of policy-relevant outcomes?* (CALDER Working Papers). Washington, DC: National Center for Analysis of Longitudinal Data in Education Research.

Lawler, E. E., III. (2008). *Strategic talent management: Lessons from the corporate world.* Madison, WI: Consortium for Policy Research in Education.

Leithwood, K. (2013, June). *Strong districts and their leadership.* Paper commissioned by the Council of Ontario Directors of Education and the Institute for Educational Leadership.

Leithwood, K., & Jantzi, D. (2008). Linking leadership to student learning: The contributions of leader efficacy. *Educational Administration Quarterly, 44,* 496–528.

Leithwood, K., Louis, K. S., Anderson, S., & Wahlstrom, K. (2004). *How leadership influences student learning.* New York, NY: Wallace Foundation.

Levin, J., & Quinn, M. (2003). *Missed opportunities: How we keep high-quality teachers out of urban classrooms.* Brooklyn, NY: New Teacher Project.

Loeb, S., Kalogrides, D., & Horng, E. L. (2010). Principal preferences and the uneven distribution of principals across schools. *Educational Evaluation and Policy Analysis, 32,* 205–229. doi: 10.3102/0162373710369833

Louis, K. S., Leithwood K., Wahlstrom K. L., & Anderson S. E. (2010). *Investigating the links to improved student learning: Final report of research findings.* Minneapolis: University of Minnesota, Center for Applied Research and Educational Improvement.

Louis, K. S., & Wahlstrom, K. (2011). Principals as cultural leaders. *Phi Delta Kappan, 92*(5), 52–56.

Marzano, R. J., Waters, T., & McNulty, B. A. (2005). *School leadership that works: From research to results.* Alexandria, VA: Association for Supervision and Curriculum Development.

May, H., & Supovitz, J. A. (2011). The scope of principal efforts to improve instruction. *Educational Administration Quarterly, 47,* 332–352.

Melton, T., Mallory, B. J., & Green, J. (2010). Identifying and assessing dispositions of educational leadership candidates. *CAPEA Journal, 22.* Retrieved from files.eric.ed.gov/fulltext/EJ965161.pdf

MetLife. (2013, February). *MetLife survey of the American teacher: Challenges for school leadership.* Retrieved from https://www.metlife .com/assets/cao/foundation/MetLife-Teacher-Survey-2012.pdf

Milanowski, A., & Kimball, S. (2008). The principal as human capital manager: Lessons from the private sector. In R. E. Curtis & J. Wurtzel (Eds.), *Teaching talent: A visionary framework for human capital in education* (pp. 69–90). Cambridge, MA: Harvard University Press.

Miles, M. B., & Huberman, A. M. (1994). *Qualitative data analysis* (2nd ed.). Thousand Oaks, CA: Sage.

Murphy, J., Smylie, M., Mayrowetz, D., & Louis, K. S. (2009). The role of the principal in fostering the development of distributed leadership. *School Leadership & Management, 29,* 181–214.

National Conference of State Legislatures. (2012). *Preparing a pipeline of effective principals: A legislative approach.* Retrieved from http://www .ncsl.org/documents/educ/PreparingaPipelineofEffective PrincipalsFINAL.pdf

New Leaders for New Schools. (2009). *Principal effectiveness: A new principalship to drive student achievement, teacher effectiveness, and school turnarounds.* New York, NY: Author.

New Teacher Project. (2006, September). *Improved principal hiring: The New Teacher Project's findings and recommendations for urban schools*. Brooklyn, NY: Author.

Odden, A. (Ed.). (2011). *Strategic management of human capital in education: Improving instructional practice and student learning in schools*. New York, NY: Routledge.

Orr, M. T., & Barber M. E. (2007). Collaborative leadership preparation: A comparative study of innovation programs and practices. *Journal of School Leadership, 16*, 709–739.

Orr, M. T., King, C., & LaPointe, M. (2010). *Districts developing leaders: Lessons on consumer actions and program approaches from eight urban districts*. Newton, MA: Education Development Center.

Orr, M. T., O'Doherty, A., & Barber, M. (2012). *Designing purposeful and coherent leadership preparation curriculum: A curriculum mapping guide*. Charlottesville: University of Virginia, University Council for Educational Administration. Retrieved from www.ucea.org

Orr, M. T., Silverberg, R., & LeTendre, B. (2006, April 10). *Comparing leadership development from pipeline to preparation to advancement: A study of multiple institutions' leadership preparation programs*. Paper presented at the annual meeting of the American Educational Research Association, San Francisco, CA.

Paine, S. L., & Schleicher, A. (2011). *What the U.S. can learn from the world's most successful education reform efforts*. New York, NY: McGraw-Hill Research Foundation.

Pane, J., McCaffrey, D., Steele, J., Ikemoto, G., & Slaughter, M. (2010). Findings from an experiment to evaluate the efficacy of cognitive tutor geometry. *Journal of Research on Educational Effectiveness, 3*, 254–281.

Partnership for 21st Century Skills. (2011). *Framework for 21st century learning*. Washington, DC: Author. Retrieved from http://www .p21.org/storage/documents/1._p21_framework_2-pager.pdf

Plecki, M. L., Alejano, C. R., Knapp, M. S., & Lochmiller, C. R. (2006). *Allocating resources and creating incentives to improve teaching and learning*. Seattle: University of Washington, Center for the Study of Teaching and Policy.

Potamites, L., Booker, K., Chaplin, D., & Isenberg, E. (2009). *Measuring school effectiveness in the EPIC Charter School Consortium—Year 2*. Washington, DC: Mathematica Policy Research.

Potamites, L., Chaplin, D., Isenberg, E., & Booker, K. (2009). *Measuring school effectiveness in Memphis—Year 2*. Washington, DC: Mathematica Policy Research.

Price, H. (2012). Principal–teacher interactions: How affective relationships shape principal and teacher attitudes. *Educational Administration Quarterly, 48*, 39–85.

Reeves, D. B. (2009). *Assessing educational leaders: Evaluating performance for improved individual and organization results* (2nd ed.). Thousand Oaks, CA: Corwin Press.

Rice, J. K. (2010). *Principal effectiveness and leadership in an era of accountability: What research says*. (CALDER Research Briefs). Washington, DC: National Center for Analysis of Longitudinal Data in Education Research.

Rigby, J. G. (2014). Three logics of instructional leadership. *Educational Administration Quarterly, 50*, 610–644.

Robey, P., & Bauer, S. (2013). Change in university-based programs of educational leadership: How responsive have programs been? *Journal of Research on Leadership Education, 8*, 261–279.

Robinson, V.M.J. (2011). *Student-centered leadership*. San Francisco, CA: Jossey-Bass.

Robinson, V.M.J., Lloyd, C. A., & Rowe, K. J. (2008). The impact of leadership on student outcomes: An analysis of the differential effects of leadership types. *Educational Administration Quarterly, 44,* 635–674.

Scherrer, J., Israel, N., & Resnick, L. B. (2013). Beyond classrooms: Scaling and sustaining instructional innovations. *National Society for the Study of Education Yearbook, 112,* 426–442.

Scholastic. (2010). *Primary sources: America's teachers on America's schools*. New York, NY: Author.

Southern Regional Education Board. (2006). *Schools can't wait: Accelerating the redesign of university principal preparation programs*. Atlanta, GA: Author. Retrieved from http://publications.sreb .org/2006/06V04_Schools_Cant_Wait.pdf

Southworth, G. (2002). Instructional leadership in schools: Reflections and empirical evidence. *School Leadership & Management, 22,* 73–91.

Spillane, J. P., Halverson, R. R., & Diamond, J. B. (1999, April). *Distributed leadership: Toward a theory of school leadership practices*. Paper presented at the annual meeting of the American Educational Research Association, Montreal, Canada.

Spillane, J. P., & Hopkins, M. (2013). Organizing for instruction in education systems and school organizations: How the subject matters. *Journal of Curriculum Studies, 45,* 721–747.

Supovitz, J., Sirinides, P., & May, H. (2010). How principals and peers influence teaching and learning. *Educational Administration Quarterly, 46,* 31–56. doi: 10.1177/1094670509353043

Tennessee Department of Education. (2012). Teacher evaluation in Tennessee: A report on year 1 implementation. Retrieved from http://www.tn.gov/education/doc/yr_1_tchr_eval_rpt.pdf

Tomlinson, C. A., & Strickland, C. A. (2005). *Differentiation in practice: A resource guide for differentiating curriculum, grades 9–12.* Alexandria, VA: Association for Supervision and Curriculum Development.

Tucker, M. S., & Codding, J. B. (2002). *The principal challenge: Leading and managing schools in an era of accountability.* San Francisco, CA: Jossey-Bass.

Turnbull, B. J., Erikson, A., & Sinclair, B. (2011). *Implementation of the national SAM Innovation Project: A comparison of project designs.* New York, NY: Wallace Foundation.

Turnbull, B. J., Riley, D., Arcaira, E., Anderson, L., & MacFarlane, J. (2013, July). *Six districts begin the principal pipeline initiative.* New York, NY: Wallace Foundation.

Tuytens, M., & Devos, G. (2011). Stimulating professional learning through teacher evaluation: An impossible task for the school leader? *Teaching and Teacher Education, 27,* 891–899.

Vescio, V., Ross, D., & Adams, A. (2008). A review of the research on the impact of professional learning communities on teaching practice and student learning. *Teaching and Teacher Education, 24,* 80–91.

Wahlstrom, K., Seashore Louis, K., Leithwood, K., & Anderson, S. (2010). *Investigating the links to improved student learning: Executive summary of research findings.* St. Paul: University of Minnesota, Center for Applied Research and Educational Improvement.

Wallace Foundation. (2012). *Making of the principal: Five lessons in principal training.* New York, NY: Author.

Wallace Foundation. (2013). *The school principal as leader: Guiding schools to better teaching and learning.* New York, NY: Author.

Weisberg, D., Sexton, S., Mulhern, J., & Keeling, D. (2009). *The widget effect: Our national failure to acknowledge and act on differences in teacher effectiveness.* Brooklyn, NY: New Teacher Project.

Wheeler, J. (2006). *An analysis of principal turnover, distribution, and effectiveness in the state of North Carolina.* (Unpublished master's thesis prepared for Dr. Helen Ladd). Duke University, Durham, NC.

Ylimaki, R., & Jacobson, S. (2013). School leadership practice and preparation: Comparative perspectives on organizational learning (OL), instructional leadership (IL) and culturally responsive practices (CRP). *Journal of Educational Administration, 51*(1), 6–23.

INDEX

Assessments: aligning curriculum with, 22, 32; aligning standards with, 32, 33; feedback on, 35; inter-rater reliability of, 34, 35; in Learning and Teaching category, 21, 22, 25, 33–34; missed assignments and, 34; multiple measures for, 32; rigor and, 32; teacher teams and, 99; of units of study, 25

At-risk students, 55

Attendance, 30

B

Barnard Elementary School, 70

Behavior problems: creating consequences for, 50; data analysis to correct, 50, 51; data collection about, 54, 55; expectations and, 43, 46, 50, 51; referrals for, 51; reteaching to avoid, 50; student accountability for, 50, 51; teachers' discussion of, 56

Belief-based leadership, 133, 134, 137

Benchmarking success, 48, 108, 110, 111

Bias, 63, 133, 138

Branding materials, 77

Budgets: creating, 107; facilities management in, 120–121; reviewing and identifying resources for, 116–118

C

Career aspirations, 53

Career pathways, for teachers, 86

Career skills curriculum, 55

Challenges: interpersonal leadership and, 140; students' response to, 53

Change process, 140

Chekan, T., 69

Classroom practices. *See* Instructional strategies

Climate, positive: adult-student relationships in, 43–44; college aspirations and, 53; data collection about, 54; expectations for, 43; for intellectual risks, 52

Collaboration: creating structures to promote, 75; to promote teacher learning, 96; protocols for, 99; schedule for, 114

College entrance, 33, 52; goals for, 53; as part of everyday experience, 53; students' understanding process of, 53

Community engagement, 47, 58; building, 62, 63, 122–124

Community resources, 36

Community, teachers' experiences of, 58

Conferences, postobservation, 72

Consequences: creating, 50; publishing of, 51

Content teams, 81, 84, 99, 111

Corrective instruction: data analysis for, 32, 33; using multiple assessments to guide, 33

Crisis intervention teams, 55

Crisis management, 121

Critical thinking skills, 28

Cultural competency: community and family engagement in, 47; equity-focused leadership and, 133, 138; instructional strategies and, 59; positive school climate and, 44; professional development about, 58

Culture, of students: curriculum materials and, 24; in instructional strategies, 59; in recruitment process, 79; student voice and, 61; teachers' learning about, 59

Culture-building activities, 57, 58

Curricula: alignment of, 20, 22–25, 32; career skills in, 55; maps of, 22, 23, 25; reviews of, 24; social-emotional learning in, 54

Curriculum materials, 24, 25

D

Data analysis: accountability and, 30; achievement gap and, 31; to address inequities, 59; to build family and community engagement, 62, 63; to correct behavior problems, 50, 51; for corrective instruction, 32, 33; to create master schedule, 112, 114; to create professional development, 92, 96; in instructional strategies, 31; in Learning and Teaching category, 18, 21, 30–32, 34; for retention

Epanchin-Troyan, T., 18

Equity, 58, 59, 138

Equity-focused leadership, 133, 134, 138

Ethics, 55

Exit interviews, 95

Expectations: for behavior, 43, 46, 50, 51; efficacy and, 52; interpersonal leadership and, 139; in performance management, 88, 89; positive learning climate and, 43; stages of development of, 8; students' understanding of, 35; of teachers, 17, 24, 71; tenure and, 95

F

Facilities management, 107, 120–121

Failure, preventing, 37

Families: bias toward, 63; building engagement of, 62, 63; communication with, 63, 123; in creating of school goals, 109; grading practices and, 34; involvement of, in academic success, 63; monitoring of student progress by, 35; partnering with, 44, 47; in school improvement plan, 122

Feedback: for instructional leadership teams, 84; on instructional strategies, 90, 95; from leadership teams to staff, 71, 85, 91; in Learning and Teaching category, 21, 33, 34, 35; to retain teachers, 86; students' valuing of, 53; on team meetings, 98

G

Garcia, J., 44

Goal-driven leadership, 133, 134, 137

Goals, of schools: allocating resources to meet, 105; benchmarking, 108, 110, 111; creating a strategic plan to meet, 108, 109, 111, 119; creating action plans to meet, 106; creating partnerships to meet, 107; data analysis in, 108, 109; ensuring time to meet, 105; family involvement in, 109; interpersonal leadership and, 139; leadership teams in, 108, 111; personal leadership and, 133, 134, 137; reviewing progress of, 110; in school improvement plan, 108; setting priorities for, 109

Goals, of students: for college/career entry, 53; public celebration of, 53; student input in, 61; tracking of, 33

Goals, of teachers, 89, 90, 97

Grade-level meetings: to analyze data, 18, 25, 30, 33; modeling of, 84

Grade-level teams, 81, 84, 99, 111

Grading practices, 34

Graduation, 104

Group tasks, 55

H

Higgs, Carter, King Gifted & Talented Charter Academy, 17

High-achieving students, 36, 37

High-poverty schools, 7, 9–10

Hiring fairs, 77

Hiring teachers. *See* Recruitment/onboarding, of teachers

Honors courses, 22, 23

HR department, 76, 94

I

IEPs, 37

Improvement plans, for teachers, 92, 93, 95

Independent projects, 37

Induction systems, 51, 74, 82, 83

Injustices, 61

Instructional Excellence Rubric, 72

Instructional interventions: to address achievement gaps, 37; for advanced students, 36, 37; for content mastery, 19; developing, 36, 54; identifying students for, 54; to prevent student failure, 37; student participation in, 37; tracking, 37

Instructional leadership teams: aligning mission, vision, and values to, 84; clarity of roles of, 85; in distributed leadership, 84;

feedback for, 84; feedback from, 85, 91; identifying teachers for, 86; individual development plans for, 85; as leaders of team meetings, 99; in Learning and Teaching category, 22, 24; learning walks by, 85; management of projects by, 84, 85; modeling by, 85; monitoring work of, 84; professional development of, 84; in professional growth of teachers, 92, 93; roles of, 84; succession plans for, 84; in Talent Management category, 74; in teacher evaluations, 84; in teacher observations, 85, 91

Instructional strategies: cultural relevance of, 59; data analysis for, 31; development of, 96; ensuring consistency of, 92; feedback on, 90, 95; in Learning and Teaching category, 20, 26–28, 29; monitoring and reviewing of, 28

Instructional time: allotting extra, 36; maximizing, 27, 114, 115

Intellectual risks, 52

Interim assessments: aligning standards and curriculum to, 32, 33; teacher review of, 33; timing of, 33

Interim staff, 83

Interpersonal leadership, 133, 135, 136, 139

Inter-rater reliability, 34, 35

Intervention teachers, 99

Interventions. *See* Instructional interventions

Interviewing teachers, 78

L

Leaders. *See* Principals

Leadership capacity, 87

Leadership skills, 87

Leadership style, 130

Leadership teams: to assist in meeting school goals, 108, 111; identifying teachers for, 80; importance of teachers in, 69–71; in mission, vision, and values implementation, 49; in recruitment of teachers, 76, 77, 78; schedule for, 115

Learning and Teaching category: actions in, 20–37; aligned curriculum in, 20, 22–25; content mastery in, 19; data analysis in, 18;

definition of, 15; description of, 5, 15–16; examples of, 17, 18; overview of levers in, 15, 20–21

Learning outcomes: accountability of teachers in, 92; grading practices and, 34; students' awareness of, 29

Learning walks, 85, 91, 96

Lesson plans: aligning scope and sequence to, 25; allowing creativity in, 36; content of, 24, 25; instructional leadership team's review of, 91

Levers: definition of, 6; in Learning and Teaching category, 15, 20–21; in Operations and Planning category, 103–107; in Personal Leadership category, 132–141; in School Culture category, 41, 46–47; in Talent Management category, 67–68, 74–75

Low-performing schools, 2

Low-performing students, 36

M

Mastery, content: developing experiences that promote, 52; differentiated instruction and, 37; interventions for, 19; missed assignments and, 34; professional development to support, 28; to reinforce academic success, 53; standards and, 23; teachers' understanding of, 35

Mentoring teachers, 80, 83, 91, 97

Midyear evaluations, 72

Minority students: behavioral referrals for, 51; cultural competency and, 44

Missed assignments, 34

Mission: aligning instructional leadership team to, 84; benchmarking success against, 48; creation of, 46, 48; implementation of, 42; in recruitment process, 77; revision of, 49; in school improvement plan, 49

Modeling: of appropriate behavior, 50; by instructional leadership team, 85; of social-emotional skills, 50; of teacher evaluations, 94; of team meetings, 84; of unit planning, 24

Monarch Academy, 18

Physical plants, 120–121

Planning times, 99

Poverty. *See* High-poverty schools

Principal actions: definition of, 6; in Learning and Teaching category, 22, 24–37; in Operations and Planning category, 6–7, 108–125; in Personal Leadership category, 132; in School Culture category, 48–62; in Talent Management category, 76–99

Principals: as constant presence in classrooms, 92; evaluating, 11; importance of, 1, 45; low-performing schools and, 2; in retention of quality teachers, 1; school culture and, 2; self-reflection by, 141; student achievement and, 1–2; teacher effectiveness and, 2

Priorities, of school, 109, 110

Problem solving: students' use of, 29; in team meetings, 99; in units of study, 25

Professional development: action plans for, 30; analyzing data to create, 92, 96; calendar for, 96, 97, 114; components of, 97; on cultural competency, 58; goals of, 97; in hiring procedures, 78; for instructional leadership team, 84; participation in, 29; in performance management, 73, 75; for retention of teachers, 87; on social-emotional learning, 55; to support mastery, 28; teachers as leaders of, 70, 87, 97, 98. *See also* Teacher training

Propel McKeesport Charter School, 69

Public forums, 51

R

RAND Corporation, 3

Recruitment/onboarding, of teachers: creating induction process in, 82; definition of, 74; expanding hiring pool for, 76, 77; importance of, 67, 68; leadership teams' involvement in, 76, 77, 78; marketing materials in, 77; rubrics for, 69; selection criteria in, 78, 79; staff assignments in, 80, 81, 82; stakeholders' involvement in, 79; student culture in, 79; timing of, 68, 76

Referrals, behavioral, 51, 55

Reid, G., 70

Relationships, district, 107, 122–124

School culture: identifying issues in, 55; importance of principal in, 45; interpersonal leadership and, 139; principal's influence on, 2; vision and mission in, 42

School Culture category: actions in, 48–63; description of, 5, 41–45; examples of, 43, 44

School improvement plan: adult learning in, 96; community and family involvement in, 122; goals for, 108; mission, values, and vision in, 49; students' input in, 61

Scope and sequence: aligning lesson plans to, 25; aligning standards to, 23; in Learning and Teaching category, 20, 23

Self-reflection, 86, 113, 141

Social pressures, 55

Social responsibility skills, 51

Social-emotional learning skills/supports: creating values for, 48; expectations of, 51; importance of, 46; integration of, into curriculum, 54; modeling of, 50; teacher training in, 54, 55; teachers meeting to discuss, 57

Staff assignments, 74, 80, 81–82

Staff Success Statement, 69

Stages of development: characteristics of, 7–10; in high-poverty schools, 7; importance of, 10; permanence of, 9; purpose of, 7; usefulness of, 10–11

Stakeholders: building relationships with, 122; communication with, 107, 123; in recruitment process, 79; in revision of mission, values, and vision, 49; strategic plan and, 109

Standards: aligning assessments with, 32, 33; aligning curriculum with, 22; aligning scope and sequence to, 23; aligning units to, 24; mastering, 23; students' understanding of, 29; surpassing, 23

Strategic plans, 108, 109, 124

Stress management, 55

Student achievement. *See* Academic success

Student profiles, 57

Student voice: building of, 60; definition of, 47; use of, 61

Student-centered differentiation. *See* Differentiation

Substitute teachers, 80, 81

Subtractive Schooling: U.S. Mexican Youth and the Politics of Caring (Valenzuela), 44

Succession plans, 84

Summative assessments: feedback on, 35; of teachers, 72, 95

Systems and structures: addressing injustice in, 61; for behavioral infractions, 50; to build family and community engagement, 63; to induct new staff and students, 51; to maintain vision, 48; to reinforce behavioral expectations, 51; to revise mission, vision, and values, 48; stages of development of, 8

T

Talent Management category: actions in, 74–99; description of, 5, 67–73; examples of, 68, 69; levers in, 67–68, 75–76

Teacher effectiveness, 2

Teacher evaluations: data collection for, 94; examples of, 72; individualization in, 88; instructional leadership team in, 84; modeling of, 94; rubrics for, 72, 88; timing of, 75, 90, 115; using TLF for, 11; walkthroughs for, 90. *See also* Performance management

Teacher recruitment. *See* Recruitment/onboarding, of teachers

Teacher training: in family and community engagement, 62; in social-emotional skills, 54; teacher expectations and, 17. *See also* Professional development

Teachers: accountability of, for student outcomes, 92; action research by, 86; addressing lack of skills in, 92, 93; assessing strengths and weaknesses of, 92; building leadership capacity of, 87; in calendar review process, 113; career pathways for, 86; certifications of, 79; in development of other teachers, 81, 87, 97, 98; in discussion of behavior problems, 56; diverse expertise of, 76; expectations of, 17, 24, 71; improvement plans for, 92; induction systems for new, 51; interviewing, 78; in leadership roles, 69, 70, 74; in learning about and valuing of students' cultures, 59; learning walks by, 91; material review by, 25; in meetings to discuss social-emotional development, 57; mentoring, 80, 83, 91, 97; monitoring of, 26, 28; promoting learning in, 96; in recruitment process, 77; retention of, 1; review of interim assessments by, 33; self-reflection